Building
Culturally
Responsive
Classrooms

Building Culturally Responsive Classrooms

A Guide for K–6 Teachers

Concha Delgado Gaitan

CORWIN PRESS
A SAGE Publications Company
Thousand Oaks, California

For information:

Corwin Press
A Sage Publications Company
2455 Teller Road
Thousand Oaks, California 91320
www.corwinpress.com

Sage Publications Ltd.
1 Oliver's Yard
55 City Road
London EC1Y 1SP
United Kingdom

Sage Publications India Pvt. Ltd.
B-42, Panchsheel Enclave
Post Box 4109
New Delhi 110 017 India

Printed in the United States of America.

Library of Congress Cataloging-in-Publication Data

Delgado-Gaitan, Concha.
Building culturally responsive classrooms : a guide for K-6 teachers /
Concha Delgado Gaitan.
    p. cm.
Includes bibliographical references and index.
ISBN 1-4129-2618-1 (cloth) — ISBN 1-4129-2619-X (pbk.)
  1. Multicultural education. 2. Multiculturalism—Study and teaching (Elementary)
3. Classroom management. I. Title.
LC1099.D44 2006
370.117—dc22   2005031707

This book is printed on acid-free paper.

06 07 08 09 10 9 8 7 6 5 4 3 2 1

Acquisitions Editor:	Rachel Livsey
Editorial Assistant:	Phyllis Cappello
Production Editor:	Jenn Reese
Copy Editor:	Marilyn Power Scott
Typesetter:	C&M Digitals (P) Ltd.
Proofreader:	Joyce Li
Indexer:	Ellen Slavitz
Cover Designer:	Michael Dubowe
Graphic Designer:	Lisa Miller

Contents

Preface

With many years of experience in teaching, administration, and research experience, I was drawn to write this book to dispel the notion that culture is a craft or a historical image that hangs on classroom walls. Rather it is the people, their networks, and how they live their lives, as well as the interpretations of these that we make. This book is a practical resource for elementary school teachers about real culture with real teachers and educators in real classrooms and communities. Teachers, family members, and community leaders were kind enough to allow observations, interviews, and audio and video recordings in their own settings. They opened up their lives for us to learn from their particular situations, and I fully appreciate their gifts to help us learn about the possibilities of culturally responsive instruction.

About the time that I first thought about writing this book, I was in a conversation with teachers who faced serious cutbacks resulting from state and federal budgetary deficits. One of their main concerns was that curricular programs, like multicultural education, would be eliminated because of the lack of funds. The teachers complained that school assemblies, cultural fairs, and resources for ethnic cuisine and dances were on the chopping block. Though legitimate, their disquiet sounded to me as though their schools were really celebrating the "ideal" cultures of diverse ethnic groups.

The teachers' apprehension returned me to a time when I was an elementary school principal in an inner-city school where over 70% of the students were either African American, Latino, Vietnamese American, Filipino American, Native American, or Chinese American. Of the twenty-six teachers on the staff, twenty-two were European American, one was African American, one Japanese American, and two were Latino. The teachers became furious with me when I had us design a program to immerse ourselves in classes, lectures, and inservice training to understand the deeper meaning of cultural diversity. I cancelled the Cinco de Mayo cooking fest and the Chinese New Year dances until I was convinced that as educators, we knew the history and lives of the people whose holidays and festivities we celebrated.

Thinking back, it was a harsh step to take, but it did force us to engage in honest dialogue. I wanted to make clear that the cultural crafts that hung in the classrooms were part of a people's "ideal" culture and that the "real" culture was lived day by day through that group's language, their family kinships, their community social networks, what they value and believe, and the meaning that they attribute to their experience. Make no mistake—music, dance, cuisine, and holidays are integral to all cultures because they unite people; they are rooted in the meaning of people's real culture. However, when only the visible, ideal culture is spotlighted, it results in stereotyping, making exotic and minimizing people's real-life, complex experience, setting them apart from European Americans who are considered "real" Americans. People's cultural identity rests on the expression of their day-to-day values, shared language, common history, attitudes, rules, and rituals and the meanings these are given.

For many of the European American teachers in the school where I was a principal, the most surprising result of the education on culture was to learn that they too had a community. They learned that everyone has one or more cultures they participate in. Up to that point, many of them believed that only recent immigrants from other countries or people of color in the United States had cultures.

Ask any person on the street if they believe that all students deserve an equitable education and an opportunity to learn; that person will probably say, "Yes." Yet there is a fundamental incongruence between our desire to educate every student who shows up in our classrooms and the traditional way that the educational system is organized. There is no equality unless we account for our diversity in race, ethnicity, culture, gender, socioeconomic status, and learning disabilities. And of course, there are regional differences that add to the mix. In a wonderfully messy way, all of these forms of diversity intersect across each other because real life isn't easy to package. We must pay serious attention to the complexity of these issues as they pertain to learning and set a path to change the inequities. To address the issue, I center my attention on how culture and learning intersect.

Indeed, culture is integral to learning. Culture is the blueprint that determines our way of thinking, feeling, believing, and behaving. Culture also shapes our perceptions, interpretations, and forms of communication. Largely, culture defines our lifestyles. It's our identity, how we talk, our actions, gestures, how we handle time and space, and how we work and play.

For too long, notions of cultural differences have been interpreted as cultural deficits. From this perspective, groups different from European

Americans have been considered less intelligent and capable. Schools and the society at large have further perpetuated the deficit notion by comparing minority cultures against the majority culture. Such a comparison relegates culturally diverse groups to an inferior position. If a group is considered inferior, it tends to skew an understanding of those students' learning experience: when students from a minority group underachieve, educators attribute academic failure to the home culture (Laosa, 1983). When we assume that students' home culture is to blame for their underachievement, we set up an impossible problem to correct because as teachers, we cannot change the students' home life.

Culture plays a central role in the classroom. I draw from the fields of anthropology and education to construct a critical cultural perspective to inform how culture actually plays out in the daily life of classroom learning settings. Critical notions accept that culture is a fundamental process of human growth and learning (Gay, 2000; Lewis & Watson-Gegeo, 2005). Culture is fluid, negotiable, and dynamic (Foley, 1990). It is not a straitjacket or a set of fixed, permanent traits. From a critical viewpoint, culture determines the way in which new knowledge is integrated from varied sources to serve new purposes. This viewpoint differs from the deficit perspective in that it allows us to become proactive in the learning setting. It shifts our task from blaming to actually probing and reshaping the processes, policies, and contexts designed to address inequity. Ultimately, the premise is that no single culture is superior to another.

Thinking about our classrooms from a critical perspective, we can exercise our power in creating policies, contexts, and content to address conditions of those facing inequity in the classroom (Stein, 2005). Solutions to inequities of learning are found in the context and content of the classroom cultural setting.

When we define classroom culture in terms of context and content, it makes negotiation in the learning setting possible, benefiting all involved. *Context* refers to the set of relationships in which a life event is situated. Lewis and Watson-Gegeo (2005) ask us to picture concentric circles of influences, moving from the center outward, in which children and adults interact in any activity. *Content*, on the other hand, is the actual subject matter and formal curriculum which encompass the skills taught, along with the interactions that carry out the instruction (Gay, 2000; Hernández, 1997).

Culturally responsive curriculum content deals with concepts, principles, and ideas that explain power struggles, privilege of one group over another, and cultural identity (Gay, 2000). Winifred Montgomery (2001) discussed culturally responsive classrooms with respect to teaching children with exceptional needs. She described the classroom as a responsive place that contains these elements: "the presence of culturally diverse students and the need for these students to find relevant connections among themselves and with the subject matter and the tasks teachers ask them to perform" (p. 4). According to Darling-Hammond and Bransford (2005), teachers are the central figures of the cultural learning setting. They each bring a set of values and beliefs from their own cultural backgrounds.

As part of the human family, we all live in one or more cultures. The extent of our participation in our cultures defines the plan from which we proceed. We learn to become successful people by observing and participating in our cultures and society in general in the social roles that we perform, such as mother, father, child, teacher, nurse, doctor, or business person. We are influenced by the cultures in which we engage just as much as we shape our cultural environments. Our competency in a culture depends a great deal on the degree to which we participate actively in it. Thus we are all socialized according to the patterns of the culture in which we are raised. It is easy to forget that it is a constantly changing organism. We are not merely passive recipients of a culture transmitted to us; we actively create and recreate our culture. People's places of residence, identities, histories, and social contexts shape the relationship between knowledge and power (Apple, 1993; Freire, 1970, 1973; Giroux, 1992; Shor, 1992).

Although culturally responsive teaching calls for acknowledging the presence of linguistically and culturally diverse students in the classroom, a culturally responsive paradigm is imperative in all classrooms. European American students, just as students from culturally diverse backgrounds, ought to learn about the importance of other cultural groups.

In schools, we interact with many cultures day in and day out. First of all, as educators we behave, believe, and feel according to our respective cultural backgrounds, references, and preferences. Essentially, our cultures frame our total experience. Second, schools operate in a culturally bound way, given their organization, and, student-teacher interactions are rule bound. Students' and teachers' attitudes and values as well as teachers' expectations are communicated both verbally and nonverbally. Third, the student population brings a host of different cultures and languages, depending on the community. Thus in school, both students and teachers are part of the school's cultural experience; the elements are the teachers' cultural background, the students' cultural background, and the language that adults and children speak in the classroom. In a sense, teachers are cultural brokers between their students and the school culture. This is especially necessary for students who come from culturally diverse backgrounds.

In different parts of this book, I refer to cultural continuity and discontinuity, the sameness and differences within and between cultures.

Continuity is the process of cultural traditions and customs continuing in a similar way across generations and between communities or institutions, like family and school. Students for whom English is not their first language experience discontinuity if the classroom language is English only. If students speak English and are familiar with the school culture, they experience cultural continuity. Continuity is preferred, because new knowledge is more accessible and retained longer when it's connected to prior knowledge and references.

In contrast, students whose home language is Chinese, for example, will experience linguistic and cultural discontinuity until they become proficient in English. Cultural continuity and discontinuity occur in all areas of culture, including values and practices. Students are advantaged in their learning if they experience cultural continuity between their home settings and the classroom.

In a complex society, we all experience some form of discontinuity. However, students who have to perform under such conditions are disadvantaged unless there is a strong scaffolding system in place. To support students' learning, we need to acknowledge how the school and the home cultures intersect. Critical culture is in progress when there's a learning setting where students learn together across their differences.

Language is a strong component in creating a culturally responsive setting, especially for students who speak languages other than English. In reference to students who speak a language other than English, I use the term *limited English proficient* (LEP) throughout the book. For the sake of consistency, it is what is used in Title 3 of the federal No Child Left Behind Act (2002).

Designing a cultural environment in which all students can learn takes into account the totality of the cultural knowledge which they bring to school. Components of culture that matter most in creating effective learning settings include systems of language, of core values, and of behaviors that influence how daily lives are conducted. Language use and communication styles also play a part. Beyond the visible elements of culture are perceptions and meanings attributed to any given event.

Cultural identity labels assume different forms, including the boxes we check on government census forms or favorite pieces of literature. For the purpose of this book, I have chosen to identify cultural groups by using the names of their ethnicities and further identifying them as American. That is, people from other countries living in the United States are American, even though they have a different cultural origin. For Anglo or white students, I use the term *European American* because it identifies the group by their cultural origin. I do not use American after the term *Latino* because the label is a larger umbrella for people from numerous Latin

American and Caribbean countries. I also do not hyphenate American ethnic groups because some groups consider the hyphen a symbol marginalizing minority cultural group in the United States.

The book is divided into two parts, discussing (1) the context and (2) the content of the learning setting. Each chapter is organized according to the components diagramed in the following figure.

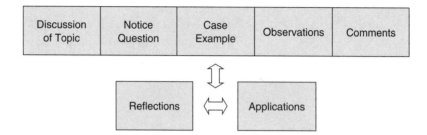

In the initial part of each chapter, I discuss the pertinent research. This sets the stage for the case example that follows. Before each illustration, I pose a question under the heading, "Notice." I want to focus attention on a specific question that can orient you as you examine the example. The case examples demonstrate how teachers, students, their families, and other educators create equitable learning settings, given the issue in each respective chapter. Following the Case Example, I share observations that to me seemed important, given my understanding of the illustration. They're not intended to be the last word on the subject, and they may not be what you will find to be the most significant. Hopefully, you will for-mulate observations specific to your perceptions and interests. The com-ment sections consist of general statements about the chapter's topic. In the reflections, readers can pause and examine their own situations. The applications sections offer ideas and opportunities to put an aspect of the topic into action.

In Part I, the Context section, I begin with the concepts of cooperation and competition because through them we get to see how the cultural ways in which children learn in their homes and community transfer to their classroom behavior. After a glimpse outside of school, I bring the focus back into the classroom in dealing with issues of policies affecting the inclusion of exceptional students and those with special needs. These two groups are subject to cultural beliefs as well as educational policies. And their access to learning settings that best meet their needs is crucial as we consider culturally responsive classrooms. Then, I move into the way the classroom furniture is arranged, not to make light of the situation but rather to visit the concept of cultural discontinuity and how something seemingly minor reflects important cultural values that influence learning.

I then travel to the students' cultural identities and the school's attempt to understand how important it is for students to maintain their connection with their home cultures. The logical next step is to look at the topic of parent education and how critical the teacher-parent partnership is to students' learning.

Part 2, the content section, follows a progression of subject matter taught in classrooms. I present the topics in the order that makes sense when thinking about teaching in culturally responsive classrooms. Each subject builds on the one before it the first chapter is about appreciating cultural differences. The chapter on building literacy expands the chapter on English language development. Then equity issues are addressed. Through these subjects, teachers increase the learning opportunities for all students. The last chapter sums up the lessons learned from teachers, students, and parents and their complex situations, which they have shared so kindly.

Chapter I—Introduction: The context section contains chapters on the cultural configuration needed to achieve academic performance. This includes how teachers organize the classroom to include students, parents, and other resources, such as policies, to make it culturally responsive. Although the classroom's physical and material props are part of learning setting, the cultural organization of the classroom contains more than desks and chairs. It also involves the verbal and nonverbal interaction that shapes knowledge. *Content* in the classroom—formal and informal curriculum—comprises the subject areas through which students and teachers interact. This substance is embedded in the cultural organization, including subject matter, lessons, and materials used in the classroom.

PART I. CONTEXT: CONFIGURING THE CLASSROOM FOR ACADEMIC EQUITY

Chapter 2—Engaging With Children's Values Around Cooperation and Competition—is the springboard for understanding how children perform in and out of their homes, play in their community and the school, and organize their lives according their familiar cultural rules. Yolanda's teacher shows how classroom lessons either engage or discount children's skills which they bring to school.

Chapter 3—Culturally Responsive Classroom Discipline—discusses how decisions get made in a culturally bound way. Teachers and school administrators have to pay attention to the school's cultural composition and the manner in which suspensions, expulsions, and afterschool detentions are issued. First-person accounts by teachers recognize that close dialogue with the students' home cultures can collaboratively resolve discipline and other behavior problems. Classroom teacher, Ms. Cohen, recognized that addressing a culturally diverse student's behavior problems meant confronting her own perceptions of cultural differences.

Chapter 4—Accelerating Exceptional Students—focuses on advancing students from all linguistic and cultural groups as part of creating a culturally inclusive learning setting. Students from diverse linguistic backgrounds exhibit their talents in significant ways. Identifying students with exceptional abilities necessitates teachers becoming involved with special programs to integrate students with diverse needs. Mrs. Zims found herself dealing not only with Hai, her student, but also with the administration, Hai's parents, and the community to address appropriate placement for Hai, who had exceptional academic skills and was bored in the classroom.

Chapter 5—Including Students With Special Needs—talks about the main goal of special education: to integrate students with disabilities into inclusive settings. Labeling students as "disabled" poses lifelong problems for students with disabilities unless they can learn in nonjudgmental environments, where teachers and peers recognize their diverse abilities. Mrs. Hansen works with a student with special needs in interactive learning environments, allowing him to use more expressive language and manage his time more independently.

Chapter 6—Culturally Responsive Classroom Management—shows how a hierarchy of power is established by the way that the furniture is organized. How and where the students sit either facilitates or discourages teacher-student interaction which in turn determines the extent to which students can maximize their potential. Teacher Mrs. Jones demonstrates the positive aspects of cultural discontinuity that builds a supportive learning environment for her students. She provides a strong learning setting, different from what students experience at home and their community, by emphasizing quiet and orderliness, allowing them to concentrate and work in an orderly fashion. Her respect and high expectation for her students validates their potential.

Chapter 7—Supporting Children's Cultural Adjustment—describes how Russian refugee students and their families orchestrate their social and cultural context as they make meaning of their daily practices. The schools provide ways in which students can grow and change. Russian students are forced to shape a new cultural identity, and that requires much more than the school curriculum. It takes the assistance and support of their families, church leadership, and other community institutions.

Chapter 8—Connecting Home and School—deals with an aspect central to the classroom's cultural process. Parent-teacher communication is founded on a set of cultural beliefs and practices that can either unify or separate these two groups. Bridging the two settings requires a common language of respect, trust, and willingness that allows parents and teachers to work toward one goal—students' academic success. Teachers Ms. Kent and Mrs. Calvo work with classroom parents to bridge families and schools by training parents in math and literacy and having some parents to co-lead parent training workshops.

PART II. CONTENT: LEARNING SUBJECT MATTER THROUGH CULTURE IN THE CLASSROOM

Chapter 9—Teaching Cultural Diversity—discusses building bridges between cultures through effective teaching, expanding students' social worlds, and motivating and celebrating the underpinnings of human justice, equity, and others' cultural values and customs. The way cultural differences are taught in the classroom can unify or create distance between students and the communities they live in. Ms. Carey broadens students' thinking about family differences and different families through quilt making and other family cultural recreation activities.

Chapter 10—Becoming Proficient in English—deals with a crucial issue. Without a doubt, instruction in English is the most pivotal part of cultural classroom curriculum. Stories abound about the way that schools hold low expectations of Limited English Proficient (LEP) students. But where strong systematic efforts are made to prepare teachers to teach English language development, their students' academic performances flourish. Ms. Rivers works with Chua and other LEP students as they attempt to learn English in a school without a formal English Language Development (ELD) program.

Chapter 11—Building Literacy—focuses on a culturally defined process involving the instruction and use of oral and written text blended into a system of communication. This combines the knowledge that teachers bring to the classroom with the ways that parents pose questions to their children and the bedtime stories that live in their memories. In his classroom, Mr. Sanchez challenges the students from culturally diverse backgrounds to wrestle with fiction and fantasy by tapping into their own worlds outside of school.

Chapter 12—Creating Equity in Math and Science—discusses how implementing peer interaction and involvement increases learning. The more students participate in their own learning, the more they learn. The promise of interactive instruction is that teachers and students learn new roles and new ways of learning, group work, for example. Interactive instruction fosters open-endedness, multiple intellectual abilities, and a common group product. It is critical to build equitable learning environments for those students previously marginalized in math and science. Mr. Beck and Ms. Williams use interdisciplinary methods to teach students the interrelationships that exist among math, language, and culture. Students learn the tools to discover explanations of their own, and they learned self-reliance through the critical inquiry method.

Chapter 13—Fostering Gender Equity—posits that gender identity is learned and advocates making the issue of gender prominent in the curriculum, the classroom routines, and school practices in general. It describes how classroom teachers are now better prepared with awareness, knowledge, and materials to teach new values to their students about the true potential of girls and women in society. Mrs. Yeh feels strongly about the importance of the subject of gender equity. Her interdisciplinary curriculum exposes both boys and girls to a rich variety of women's cultural contributions to society and the day-to-day work involved for women to break out of conventional roles and move into professional arenas.

Chapter 14—Crafting an Interdisciplinary Curriculum—builds on the reality and complexity of people's lives in this society. In elementary schools, teachers successfully combine disciplines through thematic projects and subject matter, such as literature, environmental studies, history, and music. And by doing so, they expand cultural perspectives in learning. Ms. Guy and Mrs. Jason foster respect for the Cheyenne culture. They present the multidimensional life of the Cheyenne people while motivating students to question their attitudes about lifestyles of people different than themselves.

Chapter 15—Responding Culturally in Teaching—spotlights the idea that linking culture to learning involves a rich web of knowledge of all parties involved—teachers, students, peers, parents, the wider educational system, and the broader community. Children bring to school a treasury of information about their cultures, families, and communities. By creating learning settings that integrate students' multiple abilities, intelligences, and cultural and linguistic resources, teachers set high expectations and provide equitable learning opportunities in English, literacy, math, science, and multicultural education.

The chapters in this book illustrate how culture manifests in the daily life of the classroom and how teachers play a central role in shaping school culture. They share various conscious and effective ways to harness students' cultures to enhance learning.

Building Culturally Responsive Classrooms supports teachers in their efforts to build awareness of cultural complexities and how they intersect with socioeconomic conditions, geographic settings, and gender roles. The case examples in each chapter assist teachers in designing culturally responsive classrooms by using culturally responsive, interactive teaching with students and their families and establishing school policies that respect culturally diverse groups.

My professional biography has been rich with opportunities to work with culturally diverse students, families, and communities. Although much of my professional work has been conducted in Latino communities in the southwestern United States, I have also worked with Russian refugee, Hmong, African American, Vietnamese, and Alaskan Native communities. Urban, suburban, rural, small, and large communities provide the background for this book. In my various professional roles, I have had the privilege of observing, studying, appreciating, and participating in changing learning communities for the better. Since the very first day I walked into my first classroom as a teacher, I have been interested in how the students utilized their home languages and cultures in learning. I have also had the opportunity to see how influential family life is in children's learning. The families I have met value their children's education. I have observed that in classrooms where friendly handshakes replace fences, teachers, students, and families thrive. Some of those handshakes compose the stories assembled in this book.

Acknowledgments

*B*uilding *Culturally Responsive Classrooms* includes a composite of vignettes and snapshots from several much larger research projects on sociocultural issues involving different communities. It captures the essence of themes covered here. I am indebted to the many communities, schools, and talented teachers who opened their doors for me to observe and appreciate. You unselfishly shared of your time, experience, consternations, inspiration, creativity, and dreams. I appreciate your permission for allowing me to walk into your settings with my pad, pen, and audio and video equipment. Thank you for the observations, interviews, and video recordings. Per my confidentially agreement, I use pseudonyms to protect your privacy.

The contributions of the following reviewers are gratefully acknowledged:

Dana Haight Cattani
Writer
Bloomington, IN

Michele Dean
Principal
Ventura, CA

Michael Power
Director of Instruction and Assessment
Mercer Island School District
Mercer Island, WA

Helene T. Mandell
Systemwide Director, CalState TEACH
California State University
Long Beach, CA

Carolyn A. Bishop
Regional Director
CalState TEACH
California State University, Fullerton
Fullerton, CA

Susan Stone Kessler
Assistant Principal
Nashville, TN

Timothy Reagan
Dean, Faculty of Humanities
University of the Witwatersrand
Johannesburg, South Africa

About the Author

**Concha Delgado Gaitan**, PhD, brings extensive first-hand experience and knowledge on the topics of culture in the school and academic equity for linguistic and culturally diverse students to *Building Culturally Responsive Classrooms*. Her professional experience includes positions as an elementary school teacher, elementary school principal, ethnographic researcher, and a professor of Anthropology and Education at the University of California, Santa Barbara and Davis campuses. She is the recipient of the George and Louise Spindler award for her lifetime contributions to the field of Anthropology and Education.

Given her interests in language and cultural diversity, she has worked extensively as an ethnographic researcher and collaborator in underrepresented communities. Among them are Latinos in the Southwest, Russian refugees, Hmongs in central California, Alaskan Natives in Alaska, and transnational populations in Mexico and Spain, where she has also lectured. Some of these communities appear in her earlier books: *The Power of Community; Literacy for Empowerment; Protean Literacy; Crossing Cultural Borders, School and Society*, and *Involving Latino Families in the Schools*. In *Building Culturally Responsive Classrooms*, she offers a composite of insights, instructions, and possibilities emerging from various research projects during the course of her academic career.

To Christopher, Brooke, Paul, Isaiah, Isaac Richard, Blake, and Paige.

These children comprise the next generation in my husband Dudley's and my family. Together they represent a blend of racial backgrounds. Their American, Mexican, European, African, and Chinese heritages share in the cultural wealth that makes us one family.

CHAPTER ONE

Introduction

wo major institutions have the most influence on students' learning—
the family and the classroom.

THE FAMILY

That parents are the children's first and most important teachers goes
without saying. Teachers and educators have misinterpreted this to the
point of relegating the parental role to one of supporting the school's role.
But there's more to children's home culture than meets the eye. While
teachers do not have the time to visit children's homes and observe the
parent-child interactions and other daily-life activities to get the full impact
of students' family life, children's home culture enters the classroom with
the children and is ever present.

Little attention is paid to the totality of how family culture shapes
students' academic life. Yet on the question of student underachievement,
teachers tend to hold the students' family life responsible assuming that
the family values differ from those of the school. Schools have been
described as institutions that reproduce society's culture and social
inequity (Apple, 1986; Bernstein, 1986; Bourdieu, 1977; Bourdieu &
Passeron, 1977; Carnoy & Levin, 1985). Children's academic achievement
is sometimes equated with their families' educational background, their
socioeconomic conditions, and their level of involvement in the school.
This perception assumes that families who live in lower socioeconomic
conditions are less educated and provide fewer opportunities for their
children. But although working-class and ethnically different families
often have fewer resources, precluding their involvement with their
children's schooling in the way that teachers expect, they nevertheless care

1

a great deal about their children's academic success. Generally, they have to overcome more to remain connected with their children's education (Lareau & Shumar, 1996).

To know the impact that parents have on their children's schooling necessitates taking a look at how parents support their children's learning in explicit and tacit ways. Some culturally different families may find it difficult to participate in the mainstream culture because they aren't familiar with it. Mainstream culture, with respect to the educational setting, commonly describes a classroom culture that expects certain things of students, such as to know, without being told, to remain quiet when the teacher is giving instructions. Also, they are expected to know to walk, not run, inside the classroom, to turn in their homework at the beginning of the day, and to use soft voices inside the classroom (Delgado-Gaitan, 2001).

The ways families from diverse cultural groups learn U.S. mainstream culture vary, depending on their opportunities to have contact with the majority culture. For example, ethnic groups that are native to the country or long-time residents have frequent contact with mainstream European American culture, using the same community services, stores, movie theaters, churches, and the like. Some ethnic communities are more isolated from the mainstream as a result of poverty. Recent immigrants also comprise culturally diverse communities that may be distant from the mainstream culture until they become more familiar with their new society. Some families have knowledge about the social systems in the United States prior to immigrating because they have family members who have preceded them. For those with no welcoming and orienting persons, the social and cultural adjustment may take longer.

Regardless of the length of tenure in the United States, families have their own ways of relating to their children through their cultural languages and knowledge. Few generalizations can be made about the way that parents and children relate in the privacy of their homes and how those interactions impact the children's learning. But one true thing is that the more that parents and children interact critically and positively, the better it is for children's intellectual development (Heath, 1983).

THE CLASSROOM

The school context consists of all of the individuals involved in the learning setting, the school policies that govern it, and its material resources, including the classroom furniture. The school culture encompasses the way that visitors are welcomed, how school personnel communicate with each other and the rules enforced for the students. The classroom can be described as a microcosm of society. It is composed of physical space (the arrangements, the people) and emotional space (a system of rules and expectations and interactions).

As previously mentioned, cultural manifestations in the classroom are embedded in multiple components: the teacher's cultural background, the students' cultural backgrounds, the school policies that govern the classroom, the formal textbook curriculum, the teacher-student interaction, and the language used to conduct the business of learning. How culture is learned varies on the traditions of the particular culture, and in schools, teachers have historically been the dominant figures in passing on the culture to students. This process is called *cultural transmission* and the teacher is the cultural transmitter. With the teacher in this role, the classroom is organized according to certain values, symbols, and beliefs.

Teachers are carefully trained to fulfill the role of official cultural transmitter, and professional training institutions are also organized according to certain values and beliefs. The notion of independence governs much of the classroom cultural pedagogy. For example, students are expected to do their own work without consulting others. In this way, teachers design classroom rules and pedagogy that value independence. How values are interpreted and organized varies according to each teacher's professional preparation, personal experience, and cultural beliefs.

In a setting where the teacher assumes a position of sole authority, students implicitly get the message that their ideas only matter when the teacher requests them to recall the information that was provided. At one point in the history of education, it was possible for students to learn a set of facts and a body of information and to reflect that knowledge in a single test. However, in recent decades, access to information has vastly increased through technology, as we've all experienced, making the world seem smaller and the body of knowledge overwhelming. This change has myriad implications for the classroom: the way that teachers arrange seating, what students are expected to learn, and the kinds of interaction between teacher and students and between peers. Requiring individual students to recall a single body of facts is incongruent with the changing world of complex ideas. Instead, students can learn that their ideas are valued and contribute to the collective knowledge of the classroom. Crafted correctly, pedagogy can appropriately utilize the students' voices to promote awareness and understanding of their reality as much as possible so as to create personal and collective transformation.

Learning in the classroom involves active interaction between the teacher and students. The intricate relationship between teachers and students centers around the decisions made regarding the type of instruction, the choices of curriculum, the methods of delivery of knowledge, and the way that students are challenged to think critically. Implicit and explicit values are imparted in the process.

Context: Configuring the Classroom for Academic Equity

A typical learning context is composed of individuals, including teachers, students, and parents, and the verbal and nonverbal engagements in which learning occurs. Context is teacher constructed. It is how teacher-student and peer interaction is organized. In a culturally responsive classroom, student work groups are arranged so that they provide all students the opportunity to engage in shared inquiry and discovery. It crafts the physical and visual intersection between culture and learning.

Central to academic performance is the process of incorporating students' experience in the day-to-day instruction. In the classroom, teachers arrange and manage their settings to accommodate and maximize students' abilities. Context also involves creating cultural discontinuity and continuity in supporting learning. By setting high expectations, teachers may create appropriate discontinuity. Or teachers may also create appropriate continuity by incorporating the home languages and cultures of new students and educating their parents about the school culture.

Creating culturally responsive classrooms involves allowing students to maximize their language and other intelligences. Bulletin boards and books can carry visual representations of students' ideal cultures.

Therefore, in order to create culturally inclusive classrooms, the students' family and community contexts need to be integrated into the instructional context. When this occurs, students are better able to participate more meaningfully in the learning process and succeed academically (Beals & Hoijer, 1965; Heath, 1982; Moll, 1990; Moll & González, 1997; Spindler, 1987; Trueba, 1999).

Bulletin Boards. . .

Represent current news

Show photos of community leaders from culturally diverse backgrounds

Classroom Books and Materials. . .

Include a variety of fiction and nonfiction books

Include culturally diverse computer programs

Interactive Classroom Learning Involves. . .

Students with different academic skills working together

Students of different genders, cultures, and language backgrounds sharing in activity completion

Content: Learning Subject Matter Through Culture in the Classroom

Figure 1.1 shows how content can use and unify the various cultural elements found in every classroom. Generally, the subject matter and how it is taught in the classroom embodies a set of values and beliefs that play

Figure 1.1

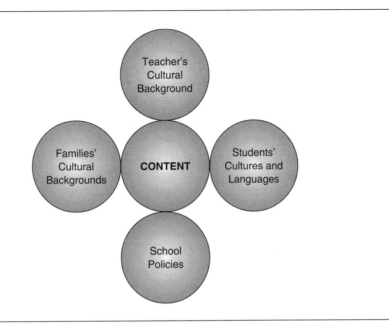

a role in students' learning. Differences in learning are a fact. Research tells us that how those differences manifest in a classroom varies, depending on the students, their home socialization, and peer groups. The language that children learn to speak before they enter the classroom, the values they learn in home interactions, and peer play activities all contribute to children's knowledge and skills that bear on how they learn in the classroom. Before students even step foot in a school, they have lived as part of a family, a community, and a social group. From them, children learn attitudes, norms, beliefs, experiences, and aspirations which they express and practice. Some students have participated in the larger mainstream culture while others have been more socially, culturally, socioeconomically, or geographically isolated.

Although cultural similarities exist among people from the same cultural group, gender, social class, regional, and individual differences also exist. It's important not to stereotype children's behavior.

Knowledge of other cultures broadens perspectives of diversity in the classroom. Students' cultural background provides teachers with a fuller picture of students' multiple skills that contribute to their learning. Incorporating culturally different approaches in instruction calls for understanding the cultures represented in the classroom and the ways of learning that take place in the children's homes.

PART I

Context

Configuring the Classroom
for Academic Equity

CHAPTER TWO

Engaging With Children's Values Around Cooperation and Competition

> **I recall . . .**
>
> When I taught fifth grade, I had a Tulalip Indian student, James, in my class. It didn't take long for me to notice that he was very quiet whenever we had class discussion. We didn't have other Tulalip or even other American Indian children in the school. His family had moved into the area so his father could take a new job. At first, I thought James was shy and that it would take a while for him to feel comfortable. So I gave him time. I didn't figure a bit of silence was pathological, since he appeared to be intelligent as he did fine on tests. I did try to encourage him by asking him specific questions that I felt confident he knew the answers to.
>
> Finally, I made a home visit to the family, figuring that I could get more information by learning about his home life. His mother and I talked about my concerns—that he did not participate in class discussions even when I encouraged him. She listened, bouncing her six-month-old baby on her lap. When I was through, she responded by telling me about where they lived before having to relocate. They had lived in a small town near the Reservation, with lots of waterways. It was a different pace of life. It was peaceful. She also said that she and her husband always told their children to be respectful to the teacher and listen carefully: They could learn more by listening than by talking. She agreed to talk with James and encourage him to talk in class during discussion.

(Continued)

(Continued)

> I thanked her for talking with me about her son and invited her to come to class and share with us some part of their culture. She said she'd think about it.
>
> I left their home with a better understanding about James's behavior. James was only playing out what he had heard reinforced in his home: to be a good learner, he had to be a good listener. It took a long time before James felt comfortable enough to participate in class discussion. I too had to be respectful that he was learning in his way and not judge him for not following the class program. James hadn't just moved from a small town to a larger city, he had literally changed cultures.

Many of us can recall an instance in the early years of school when the teacher caught us looking at another student's paper and said in a threatening voice, "Do your own work!" On the face of it, this is a reasonable request. After all, why wouldn't you expect that? But this scenario points to an underlying mainstream cultural value that regulates much classroom curriculum: independence. Teaching independence carries a great deal of weight, but teaching practices that favor some students fail others. Teachers foster familiar values that they believe are necessary to impart. And to be sure, nothing is wrong with students from noncompetitive cultures learning to be competitive. When children break classroom rules, teachers need to step back and observe the children's strengths and skills that may reflect other values. In this chapter, we step into the world of a group of children playing and learning in and out of school. They show us how they use the cultural rules that govern their interactions and relationships to learn.

What does an activity such as sharing answers with other students mean to the different people in the classroom? While we cannot deny the importance of teaching students to work independently, classroom lessons are generally organized to teach mostly competitive skills. But students from diverse cultures draw on other skills that foster their learning. Given that personal and cultural bonds with family and community are extremely strong, students naturally learn the values inherent in interactions with peers and parents. This does not prevent them from learning new ways of interacting. Such cultural discontinuities are common when students come from households where their relationships with family members and friends are based on their traditional culture. When children from diverse cultures come into contact with the mainstream teachers in the classroom, their language, behavior, and practices are likely to be judged and evaluated according to mainstream culture.

What teachers cannot see is the way that children's play and home tasks bears on student learning behavior. If teachers are unfamiliar with the students' cultures, they may believe the stereotype that culturally different children are naturally cooperative. Teaching based on this limited notion limits children's opportunities while teachers attempt to increase their curriculum.

Classroom tasks sometimes differ from home and play activities in the values that are taught through interactions. For example, daily interactions which children have with their parents impart profound values about such issues as leadership, teamwork, and competition. By the time children go to school, they already have a deep sense of what they believe and value, even if they do not express it verbally. How students' home and play interactions away from school influence their learning in the classroom can be seen in the following examples taken from an eighteen-month study of children in and out of school.

To get some insight into how children learn to work together and simultaneously challenge each other, let's take a look into Pedro and Yolanda's world—their home, school, and community in an inner city. Pedro and Yolanda can shed light on some instructional implications of peer interactions as well as teacher-student interaction in Yolanda's first-grade classroom.

CASE EXAMPLE

At Home

Yolanda and Pedro's mother, Mrs. Islas, was going to the store, leaving the sister and brother at home with a list of instructions for cleaning house and caring for Sabrina, their one-year-old sister. Yolanda was left in charge. (Their communication is translated from Spanish.)

> *Notice . . .*
>
> *What qualities does Yolanda exhibit at home and in play that can assist her classroom learning?*

Mrs. Islas: All right, Yolanda, I'm leaving, and when I return, I want this house clean. And don't leave Sabrina unattended. And don't make her cry.

(Mrs. Islas leaves. Pedro picks up Sabrina and rocks her while Yolanda washes dishes.)

Pedro: You have to wash dishes.

Yolanda: No, you do it, and I'll take care of the baby.

(Pedro puts Sabrina on Yolanda's lap and goes to sit down again for a minute.)

Pedro: Ha ha. I'm just going to give Sabrina milk and you have to wash dishes and do the rest.

Yolanda: I don't care. My friends and I are going to the park and you're not going because you have Sabrina.

(Yolanda pushes a kitchen chair up to the sink and washes the dishes. Pedro holds Sabrina on his lap and feeds her warmed-up oatmeal. He cuddles and teases her as he feeds her. When Yolanda finishes the dishes, she starts out the door.)

Yolanda: You still can't go outside; you have to sweep.

Pedro: No! You do it! You have to come in before mother gets back.

(Yolanda and her friends return home before Mrs. Islas returns. They invite Pedro to join them in a card game.)

Their mother had entrusted Yolanda with caring for her brother, the younger sister, and the household chores. She accepted the responsibility and followed through with their mother's instructions, but she delegated part of the work to Pedro. She knew just how far to push him until he refused to work and forced her to negotiate the assignment. Although Yolanda and Pedro did not collaborate in completing their tasks, they shared the total workload.

At Play

Pedro and Yolanda live near many children who attend the same school. This mostly Latino, Spanish-speaking community is home to children of all ages. Three neighbors, Herlinda, Nora, and Laura, come to Yolanda and Pedro's home and invite them over to play. Listening in as they play cards, we can see how the children play collectively, even in games which ordinarily have clear-cut winners and losers. This card game takes place in Nora's living room with Nora, Yolanda, Herlinda, and Pedro as players.

Nora brings out the cards and places them on the carpet as the others sit around her. In this card game, the children each have to match a pair of cards or lose their turn. When they get a match, they can take a second turn.

Herlinda: First!

Nora: Second, second, second.

Yolanda: Ok. I'm third.

Pedro: It's my turn now.

(They play until all of the cards are matched in pairs. Then they count how many they've each gotten. Whoever has the most cards will start the next game.)

Nora: I've got four pairs.

Herlinda: I have the most pairs. Then Pedro is second, Nora is third, and Yolanda is fourth.

Yolanda: New game!

Herlinda: I'm first because I had the most pairs.

Yolanda: I'm second. Herlinda, look, you have your pairs over there. You moved them.

Nora: Oh look, another pair.

(She picks up a pair, looks at her stack, counts her pairs, and then hands Yolanda one pair.)

Pedro: Yolanda has six pairs.

(Herlinda takes her turn.)

Herlinda: Oh look, two pairs. Here, Nora, take one pair. You only have a few.

(Nora takes the cards that Herlinda offers to her.)

Herlinda: I think I have the most pairs.

Yolanda: No, you don't. I do. The end! Now, I have eight pairs and Herlinda seven, Pedro six, and Nora four. So I'm the first winner, and you won second, third, and fourth.

(The four players begin another game, their turns determined by their winning places in the previous game. At the end of each game, Yolanda makes sure that they all have places as winners.)

In the Classroom

Yolanda attends school with many of the same children she and Pedro play with away from school. Yolanda's first-grade teacher, Mrs. Olivera, regularly divided her class into groups for math and language arts instruction. While she worked with one group, other groups were assigned independent workbook activities which they were expected to complete.

In the classroom, Yolanda's interactions with her peers reflected the values of the home culture. The students attempted to follow the teacher's expectations but quickly resorted to their familiar ways of relating to each other. When left alone, they tried to work independently, but they couldn't resist sharing with each other, and they usually found a way to do it even if the teacher disapproved, as demonstrated in the next part of the story:

> Following the opening sharing experiences, Mrs. Olivera asked the students to go to their respective workplaces. One group went with her, and they sat at a corner table. Another group went with the teacher's assistant to another corner. Yolanda's group of three girls and two boys sat together and were to work independently, but they were in the teacher's line of vision.
>
> When Yolanda finished her work, she went over to the boys' side of the table for a few moments and then watched the two other girls working. She stood by them for a few seconds and then told them they were doing the workbook page incorrectly, and she said, "Can I help you?" and she showed them her completed page.
>
> At this point, Mrs. Olivera looked up and saw the girls copying from Yolanda, and she came to their table. Speaking to Yolanda and looking disapprovingly at the other girls, Mrs. Olivera said, "You're not supposed to give them the answers. Now you're all going to have to do it again."
>
> The girls looked at each other, and when Mrs. Olivera walked away, they got fresh pages and all began again.

There was a congenial atmosphere in this classroom, but it appeared that the children in Yolanda's group were not trained to teach or explain material to each other. Sharing knowledge is a skill which Yolanda has transferred from her home and play culture. The prevailing attitude about individual work was rather competitive between the boys: They made a game out of filling in their math sheets as they asked each other for answers, then they raced against each other to finish first, with almost no regard for the concepts on the paper. The two girls in the group, on the other hand, did not participate in the contest to finish first but worked alone until Yolanda showed up and advised them of the wrong answers. Yolanda's willingness to repeat the assignment illustrates her willingness to follow the rules.

Mrs. Olivera practiced the belief that she shared in an interview—that each child has to learn how to do his or her own individual work. If anyone is caught cheating, they have to repeat the assignment.

Observations: In the classroom lesson, Yolanda plays out the skills which she learned at home and in her play activities with her peers. She has good leadership skills. She works collectively and collaboratively, in spite of the classroom rules. The cultural discontinuity between the classroom rules and Yolanda's home and play skills make it difficult for her to share her knowledge and help the others negotiate their assignment.

Comments

Children bring to school ways and skills that they learn at home, at play, and in their communities. Yolanda's collective practices in home and peer activities allow for fairness, turn taking, and egalitarian relationships among siblings and peers. The children in these interactions unquestionably have the potential to make the transition from their familiar cooperative orientation to the more competitive structures in the classroom. However, competition alone also generates defeating pressure, exclusion, and discomfort that discourage students from exercising their full strengths. When students are forced to work without support in their learning tasks, they miss out on learning in activities that promote teamwork.

Yes, Yolanda, her brother Pedro, and their peers are socialized to share home activities and support each other. These cultural rules and behaviors translate to more collective skills. However, the children also relate competitively. It is critical to incorporate students' knowledge and strong multiple skills in their learning activities. When provided with a diverse instructional setting involving cooperative and competitive learning, they rise to the expectation.

APPLICATIONS

▌Application 1

Analyze the rules in your classroom for the values that they promote. Share this information with colleagues to learn how other teachers transmit culture and how they can shape it by utilizing students' abilities to construct a learning setting that allows more cultural continuity.

▌Application 2

Consider the values inherent in the games and play activities in your classroom and in the school. What play customs do children bring? Provide opportunities for students from other cultures to share their traditions with peers.

REFLECTIONS

Reflection 1

How would a classroom setting that allows collectivity benefit students of all learning levels?

_____

_____

_____

_____

_____

_____

Reflection 2

Think about your early grade school years. What classroom rules do you recall? How did those rules support or discourage your learning?

_____

_____

_____

_____

_____

CHAPTER THREE

Culturally Responsive Classroom Discipline

I recall . . .

One year I taught second grade in a school that strongly encouraged teachers to make home visits when conducting teacher-parent conferences in order to involve the many parents that did not attend the conferences. I decided that rather than wait until parent-teacher conferences, I would meet all of the families in their homes two weeks before school began. During the visits, I explained my classroom expectations and solicited their commitment—so that the students would know that their parents and teacher were on the same page. During the year, I maintained strong connection with the parents on a regular basis by phone about their children's progress. However, it wasn't until halfway through the school year that I made an observation: our classroom did not have discipline problems that had to be referred to the counselor or the principal. Inadvertently, what I had done was to device my own discipline policy: Engaging the parents to work along with me on their children's schooling made students recognize that they had both parents and teacher supporting them and expecting the most from them. After that year, it became my discipline policy to visit families in their homes before I met the students in class.

Disciplining students in class is such an automatic part of the daily program, we seldom pause to think about the imbedded culture in the behaviors we impose. Schools have policies governing teachers and staff behavior. What becomes formal policy depends on the decision to formalize what the school administration wants to manage. In some schools, almost every action is written in formal policy format. Other schools prefer to write down only general policy pertaining to major activities undergirded by legal tethers. For example, in those schools, the student discipline policy, special education placement, and the gifted and talented education referral process compose the school policy. These guidelines are somewhat controlled by state or federal law, forcing schools to clearly define how they proceed with activities that affect students.

DISCIPLINE

Discipline policies in schools typically dictate how teachers, staff, and administrators are expected to deal with inappropriate student behavior. However, violent student behavior at school or at home potentially has legal ramifications. The extent of the policies depends on the level of detail made explicit by the school.

Setting limits and consequences for students is a fundamental part of the classroom curriculum, and curriculum standards for behavior sometimes attempt to address specifics with a general sweeping policy. However, there is no single discipline policy for any given classroom or school. Beliefs about child social development ought to lead the discussion, and given that development is culturally affected, ideally, parents and educators will engage in a negotiation process.

Commercial discipline programs, which some schools adopt, are generally designed to control student behavior and help them adjust socially and behave amiably within a school culture. In these programs, some behaviors are considered defiant without any real evidence of student intent to cause trouble. Even using such programs, individual schools' decisions regarding disciplining students when they break rules are highly subjective and culturally specific. Cultures have different beliefs about ways to deal with children's defiance to adult authority. In an effort to understand how to discipline culturally diverse children in a sensitive way, school administrators may assume that all students from a particular background will act and react the same way.

In culturally diverse schools, it is difficult for the administrators and teachers to learn all of the cultural ways of disciplining children. Many teachers are quite frustrated by their inability to control all of their students' behavior. Some resort to candy enticement to reward children's good behavior. Unfortunately, the candy reward system only pacifies the student for that instant. Students eat the candy, but it does nothing to instill an incentive to learn and internalize new behaviors. Other teachers apply a one-size-fits-all discipline policy to all students, regardless of cultural background—but the ways students respond is culturally founded.

This approach sometimes creates conflict between teacher and parents. Teachers acting alone cannot always set discipline policies in culturally responsive ways without stereotyping or misjudging the students' family life. For that reason, teachers are strongly urged to approach the issue of discipline in an open discussion with parents. As teachers discuss what makes students respond and change behavior in class, parents are encouraged to share information about the disciplinary actions in the home. Only through continuous dialogue with students' families can schools implement more culturally responsive disciplinary policies.

CHARLES IN MS. COHEN'S CLASSROOM

The example that follows does not address issues of extreme behavior. Instead, Charles and Ms. Cohen are forced to deal with what appears to be a simple case of defiance. However, the situation becomes a culturally loaded issue in this third-grade classroom in Victoria School.

CASE EXAMPLE

The Setting

Ms. Cohen gives her teacher's perspective:

> *Notice . . .*
>
> *What are the contributing factors to Charles's problem that Ms. Cohen misses?*

In Victoria School, only a general policy existed to guide teachers on ways to discipline students in the classroom and the playground. Teachers had maximum autonomy to develop classroom policies or strategies so long as they adhered to the general school policy of no fighting, no violence, no hurting anyone, and no abusive language. The consequences had to involve intervention by the teacher and the parent. If discipline problems persisted, the administration would take over and either dismiss the student from the school or refer them to a counselor outside the school for appropriate therapy. This assumed that teachers had solicited the services of their own school counselor. Protocol for the reporting child abuse cases was also explicit in writing in school policies.

Ms. Cohen's describes her plan to discipline students:

I've always tried to work on the preventive end of behavior problems. I teach students to work out their differences, and that way I minimized discipline problems. It frees me up to teach. That's not to say that we don't have problems in the classroom, but kids had every opportunity to amend their misbehavior before I call their parents to report their transgressions. I usually sit them down and tell them to be respectful to each other and to take responsibility for their actions. In other words, they have to be honest with themselves and each other about what they've done and about the way they feel about it. It works well because the students know that if they come to a third party like me and I haven't seen the conflict, I might be objective, but I may not know who's right or wrong. But if they have to face each other and look in each other's eyes, they can't hide from the truth.

From the beginning of my teaching years, I was confident that I had a designed a good way of dealing with classroom discipline until one day, a simple act caused me to call a child's parents. That incident made me see how there is no sure way to cover all bases without ongoing communication with the parents and our school counselor. It was not enough for me or the families to teach children to express respect, because there are some ways that parents may deal with children that are hurtful, if we don't communicate with parents when things are going well for their kids.

Ms. Cohen describes the classroom setting:

My classroom is set up for lot of independent work as well as small-group activities. I encourage different kinds of work modes. Sometimes we do things as a whole class, like singing or reading a story together, and, of course, I give instructions to the entire class when necessary. From the beginning of the school year, I drill into the students that I expect them to treat each other respectfully. I stress that they can manage their own behavior through positive reinforcement. I expect students to have the discipline to control themselves.

During the present school year, I've had only a handful of times when I've had to call the parent to talk to their kids about their classroom behavior. And none of them have been serious problems; it's just that when they tend to be persistent problems, I do have to call the parents. But because I teach the students self-discipline, I actually have very few real problems. Charles's case taught me how complicated this question of discipline can be. For years, I worked on shaping my classroom curriculum and classroom arrangement so that I could manage student behavior.

Charles

Ms. Cohen describes Charles's behavior:

Charles Ford is an energetic African American student. One day during math instruction, Charles and his friends were talking and not getting their work done. Charles wouldn't stay seated; he just got up and wandered around and distracted others. This goes on daily with Charles, but usually he settles down when one of the students calls him on it or when I look in his direction. I've mentioned it to his mother at conferences and have written notes home with weekly reports.

In class, I've even given him permission to do his work standing up, and sometimes it works, but during this one math period, he refused to or couldn't settle down anywhere. The worst part was that he walked around poking his classmates and distracting them. I tried to get one of the students to work with him and settle him down that way, but it didn't work. Finally, I told him to stop, and he half sat down in his chair but didn't even turn his body forward in the chair completely. He kept tapping his foot, and his knee bounced up and down. He seemed anxious about something. I stopped what I was doing and went to him, and we had the following conversation:

Ms. Cohen: What's bothering you, Charles?

Charles: Nothing.

Ms. Cohen: Something is bothering you and you can trust me to tell me. I'd like to help you.

Charles: (He lowered his head.)

Ms. Cohen: Ok. If you won't talk to me and you won't stay in your seat and do your work, I have to send you to Mrs. Chavez [the counselor]. Take your work with you and maybe it'll be a better place for a while.

Ms. Cohen continues the story:

I sent him with a referral to the counselor's office and about half an hour later, she called me and said that Charles was refusing to do anything that she asked. He was also distracting others in the area. The counselor sent him to Mr. Beau, the principal, who called Charles's mother. She left work and came to take him home.

When he returned the next day, he was limping. I asked if he had hurt himself, and he just lowered his head and nodded yes. I saw him so subdued that day that I figured his parents had talked with him and that's why he was really quiet. But he wasn't finishing much of his work this day, either. He just sat there, and when he got up to walk, he looked like he was in pain. I kept him in after the students left for recess, and I asked him to show me his foot. He said it was his knee that was sore. He showed me, and his knees were red. When I asked him if he had fallen, he said that he had had to kneel on rice all evening without dinner for being bad in school.

I met with the counselor and the principal. We decided that we had to get all of the facts about the situation before reporting it to protective services. We called Charles's mother, Mrs. Ford, to come in and meet with us. She was there after school, and we met without Charles. We told her about Charles's knees and asked her to talk to us about the situation. She was clearly embarrassed, saying that she wanted Charles to respect his teachers. She said that in the past when she did this, he had repented and said that he'd never be bad again. She looked like she was going to cry. She said that her husband and Charles's four siblings all tried to help him at home with his homework. But given all of the bad reports that she receives about Charles, she felt that they had to get stricter with him. She told us that she had even taken him to the family minister to pray with Charles to remind him to do right.

I don't know whom I felt more sorry for, Charles or his mother. Mrs. Ford said that none of her other children had been this difficult. Their teachers didn't give her bad reports about them. When Charles's mother said that, it occurred to me that somewhere in my mind, I had made some grand generalizations about African American children and their parents' expectations. Mrs. Ford went on to say that Charles was a loving son at home, but his behavior at school was such a problem. Mrs. Ford looked at us and then she gasped, realizing that we might turn her into the police and take Charles from her. Then she began to cry, telling us that she didn't want to hurt Charles. She just wanted to make him understand how important school was and how he had to respect his teachers.

Mrs. Chavez, the counselor, spoke to Mrs. Ford and asked very good questions about Charles's behavior at home as well as his medical history. We listened carefully and everyone took notes about her description of Charles at home.

The Parent's Perspective

Mrs. Ford explained:

We teach the children to be respectful to teachers and not to talk back when they're being scolded. We also expect the teachers to be able to control them in their classrooms. I know they have lots of students, and they can't take care of all of them. But I've told Ms. Cohen that if Charles does something wrong, I want to know. For a while, I was hearing from her almost once a week about how he was misbehaving, doing something wrong.

He doesn't have any medical problems that we know of. He's been healthy except for the bad ear infections and fevers that all kids get. All my children had the same thing. The doctor said they couldn't do anything about it; they just gave us antibiotics for his infections.

He's a good boy and we all love him, and he's been the only one of my kids that has forced me to be so strict with him, but what else can I do? We have to discipline him so he behaves in school.

Meeting Together

Charles was brought into the meeting and he talked to the adults about his behavior. He responded to the question, "What do you think is the problem with your classroom behavior?" Charles seemed perplexed about his behavior:

I don't know why I do what I do. I just can't help it. I feel like I try to sit still and not run around. I try to behave, but I always get in trouble.

Mrs. Chavez asked Charles another question: "Do you like school?" He responded, "Yeah, I like school. I like being with my friends, and it's OK, but I don't like getting into trouble."

Speaking to Mrs. Ford, Mrs. Chavez said,

Mrs. Ford, it sounds like you're trying to discipline to Charles so that he'll remember the pain and not repeat the offense. Certainly, Ms. Cohen, the principal, and I understand that you care about Charles's learning and want to cooperate with the school. Now we have to help Charles realize that we're all interested in helping him learn. If he doesn't feel that we're all on his side, then he'll start acting out to get our attention in a negative way. What I suggest that we do, if Mr. Beau and Ms. Cohen agree, is to test Charles for some specific learning disabilities which might possibly show some kind of Attention Deficit Hyperactivity Disorder (ADHD). It's not certain that he has it, but we need to make sure. That might give us some clues as to why he has had this problem for this past year. We also want your permission to test his hearing.

What Happened Next

Ms. Cohen reports on the follow-up to that meeting:

Charles got tested. The test showed that he had some hearing loss, which no one had caught. He also showed some tendencies toward ADHD, which accounted for his distractibility. The results helped us understand Charles's behavior a little better. Even when he tried, Charles couldn't settle down enough to focus on his work. I think he felt so frustrated that it made him more anxious. He was unable to stay seated and focus on one project for an extended period.

Students in my classroom have the flexibility to work out things without rigid rules: Respecting others' differences and kindness work in the classroom for the most part. It teaches children to take responsibility for their own behavior. I tried so hard not to make cultural generalizations about African American parents that I didn't realize that was what I was doing. I found out that parents interpret my communication differently if I'm only reporting their child's negative behavior. I have to keep contact with parents about the student's positive behavior, too.

Also, it was a shock to me as a teacher to learn how a student's bad behavior is possibly tied to some form of disability. I hadn't encountered that before. I always thought that misbehavior had to do with a student's defiance against the rules of the classroom and that if I just had a flexible classroom curriculum, it would solve all the discipline problems. But Charles taught me that I couldn't overlook any aspect of the students' learning when it comes to discipline problems.

Observations: Through a collective process, Ms. Cohen recognized that addressing Charles's behavior problems meant confronting her own perceptions of cultural differences.

COMMENTS

Ms. Cohen's flexible classroom culture and her expectations of students' behavior accommodated cultural differences. This affected Charles's situation. She had to determine whether his behavior was defiance or a learning problem. When Ms. Cohen confronted her assumptions and perceptions about students' cultural behavior, she was able to involve Charles's parent and the psychologist in addressing his discipline problem more holistically.

APPLICATIONS

▌ Application 1

Take notice of the discipline problems in your classroom. Analyze how they differ across your cultural groups. If you have a homogeneous classroom, you can still have conversations with students about behavior, expectations, and consequences at home and at school.

▌ Application 2

Assign your students to work in groups and have them decide how Charles's problem in this chapter could be resolved. Have them question each other about their decisions.

REFLECTIONS

Reflection 1

Explain the relationship between classroom discipline and the instructional curriculum.

_____

_____

_____

_____

_____

_____

Reflection 2

What cultural factors do you need to consider when there are recurring discipline infractions in the classroom?

_____

_____

_____

_____

_____

CHAPTER FOUR

Accelerating Exceptional Students From All Linguistic and Cultural Groups

> **I recall . . .**
>
> During a lengthy research project in a Latino community in Central California, the parents raised many issues that concerned them about their children's education. Number 1 on their list was that they wanted their children to have an opportunity to enter accelerated classes. Latino students had been excluded because of their limited English proficiency. The parents met with principals and district administrators, including the superintendent. They negotiated a plan by which gifted Latino students could participate in accelerated classes even if their language skills were not on par with their native English-speaking peers. The district educators agreed to expand the criteria to include more teacher observation and evaluation and to admit LEP students who were gifted in math. The success of this change spoke volumes to me about our general misperception that Latino parents don't care about education, much less about accelerated classes.

In the absence of national policy for educating gifted and talented students, I turn to what Ford and Harris (1999) assert: "One of the obstacles to the full development of talent in our society is that we have yet to make the most of the potential and abilities of racially and culturally diverse students" (p. 2). The issue is about achieving social and educational equity for gifted students from culturally diverse families.

Identifying gifted and talented children involves cultural values (Baldwin, 2004). Concerns encompass what intelligence is, who is gifted and talented, and what behavior is expected of a gifted student. Generally, gifted and talented students are those who display exceptional abilities in academic subjects or the arts. An issue within the gifted education arena is that students are usually identified through standardized IQ tests and teacher nomination. The criteria for admitting gifted and talented students into accelerated classes often excludes students from linguistically and culturally diverse groups; if culturally diverse students speak limited English, they're usually not considered as gifted and talented as their English-speaking counterparts. English language learners do not do well on standardized tests. Another possibility is that teachers may not expect students from different cultural groups to be gifted because their language skill limits the visibility of their talent. However, with parent and community pressure, some school districts have revised their policies and school criteria for accepting students into gifted education. More culturally encompassing processes rely on teachers' decisions for placing students into accelerated classes.

In designing appropriate learning settings for gifted and talented students, teachers need to differentiate their role from the curriculum. Teachers are not the only dispensers of knowledge. Rather, they are organizers of learning opportunities. Accommodating the interests and abilities of gifted and talented learners in the classroom advances their learning opportunities. Gifted students thrive in a learning environment that is rich with peer interaction and self-expression. As managers of the learning process, we teachers have a responsibility for incorporating techniques and materials to motivate and enhance their learning styles. Cognitive development is stimulated when students are able to express themselves fully. Peer interactions create and recreate classroom formats to provide a wide variety of opportunities for students to learn from each other. Students can be personally engaged in their learning by sharing interests and knowledge of specific topics and related curriculum.

Effective learning environments enable students to discover the bridges between ideas and their application. Broad-based pedagogy encompasses independent and critical thinking processes for students to respond at a higher level of thinking. Practical learning activities, such as identifying underlying problems, brainstorming, researching, and developing written reports, enhance thinking skills. But more important are lessons that motivate students to conduct independent investigations of real-world problems. These products can be achieved through exposure to learning opportunities developed within the classroom or through external environment. Inherent in these learning activities are values of how gifted children learn. They are expected to be more analytical, learn more independently, and think more abstractly and critically than regular students. Limited English Proficient (LEP) or English-proficient students who are culturally different can indeed be academically gifted. To properly identify them, a wide range of student performance assessment practices is called for, such as rubrics, portfolios, and checklists.

Organizing learning centers, study areas, computer stations, and varied work areas challenges gifted students through artistic and scientific discoveries. In the classroom, these environments allow for freedom of movement. Out of the classroom, students require additional resources, including libraries, gymnasiums, auditoriums, laboratories, music halls, and museums.

Some educators and parents have questioned why the setting for gifted students would be any different than for regular students. After all, aren't teachers supposed have the same high expectations and provide an optimal learning environment for all students, regardless of their IQs? Some parents and teachers believe that gifted students belong in isolated classrooms. Others believe that all students deserve the same accelerated learning environments where all students are challenged to learn to their optimum potential.

In the following example, Mrs. Zims, the teacher in a large, urban, fifth-grade classroom, helps us understand what it takes to deal with exceptional, culturally diverse students who speak a language other than English.

CASE EXAMPLE

The Teacher's View

Mrs. Zims explains the situation from her perspective:

> *Notice . . .*
> *What are Mrs. Zims's realizations relative to Hai's cultural background?*

When I first began teaching, we didn't have this accelerated educational policy in place. I think it's a good think that we have it now, but we still haven't really dealt with the question of identifying children from other language groups or ethnic groups who may be gifted but don't score high enough in the standardized tests to get placed in accelerated classes. My problem was that I didn't even think that some students could be gifted. I really thought that their poor performances were due to the opposite—that they were disabled. I'm embarrassed that I was so caught up with just labeling students because that's what we're supposed to do—label, evaluate, and place.

The situation involved Hai Phuong, a Vietnamese-speaking student in my class, who, by my observations, was not interested in learning and was actually rather disinterested. He had been in our school about two years, in all-English classrooms. There were other Vietnamese students in my class, and he did socialize with them in the playground but not in class.

In class, he just didn't seem to want to finish the assignments, and when I talked with his parents, they said that he didn't show any interest in homework but that he was a good kid. So I didn't have much to go on except to help him in whatever way I could.

I changed his reading group, putting him in a lower group so that he could experience success and feel good about himself. It occurred to me that maybe Hai didn't like school because he didn't feel successful. With all my heart I wanted to do whatever I could to help him feel interested and to do well. But when I moved him into the lower group, I noticed that he became almost angry. His behavior changed, not for the better but for the worse. This once-bored kid that would just sit there actually became hostile in the way he talked to other students and to me.

One day, his morning reading group was putting away their workbooks, and I called Hai to come to my table so that I could go over his completed pages. He just kept putting away his books and wasn't responding to me. Then I called him again and said, "If you don't want to deal with it now, you can stay in during recess, but I'd rather you came right now." Hai came and brought his workbook with him. He threw it on the table and it flew across to me. It messed up my stack of papers and pencils. I stood up and told him that he'd better come and pick up that workbook and my things, too. Hai did. Then he mumbled in a low voice under his breath, "Stupid thing."

I asked, "What did you say?" He turned to me and answered, "None of your business." I was getting pretty mad and told him that he was going to stay in during recess for being disrespectful. I was determined to walk over to the office and make him call his mother.

But when all the students went out for recess, I think we both cooled down, and instead, I asked him what the problem was and why he was acting so belligerent. He said that he didn't know. I believed him, and so I got concerned enough to wait until the end of the day and just try not to pressure him. After school, I met with our school psychologist, Mrs. Rhomer, and explained Hai's case. She asked to meet him before getting a formal evaluation on him.

The Student's View

Hai tells his side of the story (translated from Vietnamese):

I told my mother that I didn't want to return to school, that I hated school and that I couldn't take being so humiliated in that stupid classroom. She said that the teacher was trying to help me, but I was bored and the teacher thought I was dumb. I knew more about math than the teacher, but she never let me show how much I could do 'cause she put me in some dumb low group. I know that she thinks that because I don't speak English very well.

Anyway, I told my mother that I didn't want to go back to that classroom. She knew I meant it and that I wasn't just trying to get out of doing the work. See, here at home, I help both her and my father with the bills and the legal stuff they have to do. I don't know why, but I know what they're supposed to do and so they take me to translate sometimes. She knows I don't like staying home 'cause I like learning. It's OK. I don't like doing the school stuff, but I don't mind learning other things, except they don't teach them in school. I have some books that my cousin gave me. They're about sports and games and stuff that I like. See, everything we're doing in that class I know already, and nobody believes me so I just stopped doing it, and they think I'm dumb.

So my mother said that she and my father would go to the school and talk with them. But she did get mad at me when the teacher told her that I had thrown a book at her. And I didn't throw it at her. I threw it on the table, so it made me more mad that she told my mother that I threw it at her, and I didn't.

Mother, principal, and psychologist meet; Mrs. Zims explains:

I told the principal and the psychologist that I thought there was a problem with the classroom where Hai was placed. I though maybe he needed to be transferred. I just thought that if he went to a different teacher, he might feel better about learning. I told them too that he was bored and that if he had a change of teacher, maybe he could shape up. He's just not enjoying school and that's not like him. I've never known him to say he's bored day after day.

Mrs. Smith, the principal, and Mrs. Rhomer, the psychologist, gave me a very unexpected report about Hai. Mrs. Rhomer said that she had a Vietnamese translator to talk to Vietnamese-speaking students. The translator had talked to Hai in Vietnamese and tried to get him to talk about what was bothering him. Then Mrs. Rhomer tested him in some of the higher-level reading and math with the assistance of translator. Mrs. Rhomer found that Hai was an excellent student in both reading and math when he had a Vietnamese trans- lator assist him. He was years ahead of his own fifth-grade level. She said that if he spoke more English, she would recommend that he be tested for placement in accelerated classes. She thought that he was a good student in math.

This was a very different report than I ever imagined. I'm sure they must have noticed that I had tears in my eyes. I saw Hai so upset about school that I was afraid that he had some kind of learning prob- lem like I had heard my friends talk about in their kids.

Mrs. Phuong, Hai's mother, expresses her thoughts (she is most com- fortable speaking Vietnamese, so all of her quotes have been translated from that language):

Mr. Smith offered to transfer Hai to another class. It was a combina- tion class with fourth and fifth graders there in the same school. But after what the psychologist told me, I thought that it would be harder for Hai to be with students in the fourth grade if his ability was so much higher. They both explained that Hai still had to learn more English. I told them that Hai also knew he needed to learn more English and that we all knew he was a bright boy. So why should he be held behind until he learns more English? What I think is that they just thought that they could make me feel better by telling me how intelligent Hai was. Maybe that way, I'd stop complaining. But I told them that I wanted Hai to have the same advantage that English- speaking students have who are placed in accelerated classes. They told me that they did not have a bilingual accelerated class. And I said that my son understood the material in English if he was placed in a class that pushed him. But he also needed a Vietnamese-speak- ing tutor who could help him sometimes.

The meeting was very important for me because I too learned that my son had a good reason for behaving like he did. But I also learned that I felt strongly about getting the best placement for Hai—one that would help him to get ahead, and I knew that the options they were giving us were not going to work. I also realized that I hadn't thought about this question of speaking Vietnamese but learning in English. But at that meeting, they said that Hai would not get into accelerated classes because only gifted English speakers were allowed in that program. This upset me. So when I realized that they were only giving me two options for Hai and neither called for placing him in more challenging classes, I left the meeting. I told them that I would talk to my husband and Hai before making the decision.

Mrs. Phuong continues the story:

After telling my friend about the result of my meeting with the principal and psychologist, she suggested that I go talk with Mr. Green, an English teacher who knew my family and was also part administrator. I figured he could help me to know what my rights were in getting the right placement for Hai.

Mr. Green explained to me that the policy that allows English speakers into the gifted program excludes students who are English learners. Mr. Green also clarified that the bigger reason for not admitting English learners was that the policy called for students to be tested in a standardized IQ test and they had not looked into the possibility of finding such a test for students speaking other languages. So they didn't want to just let English learners enter accelerated classes without a standardized test. It wasn't enough to allow them to enter only because the teacher said that they were smart enough to be in the accelerated classes.

Involving the VCP

In the school district, the Vietnamese Parent Committee (VPC) had been in existence for more than one year. Vietnamese parents had educated themselves about their children's schooling, and they forged a support system to assist each other in being stronger advocates for them. All the parents spoke some English, but their meetings were always held in Vietnamese. Here Mrs. Phuong presented the problem of Vietnamese-speaking students being excluded from the gifted program. An excerpt follows from the meeting where Mrs. Phuong spoke to five of the leaders of VPC. She told the whole story of Hai's problem with school then tells of the psychologist and principal's refusal of her son to go to gifted classes. (All the dialogue is translated from Vietnamese.)

Mrs. Phuong: They told me that English learners who didn't speak English well enough could not go to gifted classes because they didn't have a Vietnamese test. They couldn't be admitted only if the teacher recommended.

Mr. Tran:	I've been talking with Mr. Green about this problem, and he's explained to me that the problem is that the educators don't see that our Vietnamese children are intelligent in a subject if they're limited in English.
Mrs. Dang:	They think language and intelligence are the same and so only English speakers are able to go to gifted classes. They've told me the same about my daughter because her English is limited.
Mrs. Phuong:	Can't you as VPC talk to them and see if they'll let Vietnamese students get into gifted classes?
Mr. Le:	We need to meet with the superintendent and the rest of them to discuss this. It isn't just Mrs. Phuong's son and Leader 2's daughter.
Mr. Lam:	They have to understand that our children are intelligent, too. Even if they speak Vietnamese and are limited in English, they're smart.
Mrs. Phuong:	What upset me was that they want my son to stay in classes that don't challenge him just because his English is limited. He could be learning so much more math and feel excited about going to school in a class like gifted. I think he deserves at least to have a chance to try it.
Mr. Ngo:	I hear that they tell Vietnamese parents that they can't place students in gifted classes because if the student fails that they'll feel bad about themselves.
Mrs. Phuong:	Hai couldn't feel worse about himself then he does now. He's so demoralized about school, it's sad to see him like this.
Mrs. Dang:	I think our kids feel better when the teachers and us, their parents, have high expectations of them. I know my children do.
Mr. Ngo:	Let's find a date so we can call the superintendent's secretary and have them set up a meeting with everyone involved.

VPC Meets With District Administrators

The VPC leaders and Mrs. Phuong met with the superintendent, the school principal, the psychologist, Mrs. Zims, and Hai's teacher. The meeting was held in English even though the parents with limited English spoke more slowly. Mrs. Phuong presented the case from the parent's perspective. The VPC leaders added their desire for the district and school policy to incorporate English language learners. Mrs. Rhomer, the psychologist, presented a summary of the problem from the administration's perspective:

Mrs. Rhomer:	Yes, it's true that Hai and other LEP students are very intelligent and can be in gifted classes, but we don't have the components or programs in place to make it possible for them to benefit from accelerated classes.
Mr. Summer (Superintendent):	I have been apprised of this problem. And I see the complexities involved in terms of the placement and teaching process where English language learners are concerned. However, I see what VPC has discussed, too. And it's important to consider that those students who have been excluded also have a right to be served. I think that's our job as administrators—to find a way.
Mrs. Smith (Principal):	Are you saying that we are supposed to accept students in gifted classes based only on teacher nomination?
Mrs. Zims:	Well, I've talked to Mrs. Rhomer about her observations and the preliminary tests she conducted with Hai. Although I had a rough time with Hai in class, I'm willing to reconsider my observations, and I would be willing to nominate him at least for math or on a part-time basis.
Mr. Lam:	Is it possible that you can place a number of LEP students in accelerated classes to try it and see how they do?
Mr. Summer:	Yes, but because this is district policy and not just school policy that is involved, I'll have to present it to the school board for approval.
Mr. Le:	We'll be sure and attend so we can show our support and also to answer any questions if you want.

Hai in a Gifted Class

Months into the school year, Hai shares his experience being in an accelerated class:

I've been in the gifted classroom for two months. It's so different, but I like it. We have to work really hard, and I've learned so much more

English, I think. The students don't care if I speak with an accent. But it's getting better. I can read more stories in English now and write longer stories, too. It's so much more fun 'cause we get to build things using geometry and then we talk about them. We have a lot more homework too, but my parents try to help me as much as possible. Yes, I think they're going to let me stay there 'til school is over in June. But I have to keep doing OK. And I really want to stay here. So I'm working hard.

Observations: Hai's mother's advocacy helped him to get appropriate placement in a class for gifted students. Although a limited English speaker herself, Mrs. Phuong marshaled support from the parent group. She confirmed the power of a collective cultural community voice concerning access to appropriate academic placement of Vietnamese students.

COMMENTS

The educators' fuller perceptions of who is gifted and talented required a conversation, which belonged in a meeting the parents. Hai Phuong sent many messages that he needed to be more challenged in the classroom. Yet it took the advocacy of his parents, the Vietnamese Parent Committee, and supportive teachers to convince the psychologist and the principal to place Hai conditionally in the gifted program. In the accelerated class, Hai rose to the level of expectation that challenged him in math and English.

Culturally, schools make policies informed by the mainstream norms and beliefs of the administrators and educators in charge of the accelerated programs. Language plays a major role in the way that educators perceive intelligence. Just as strong is the link between behavior and intelligence. The assumption is that if students misbehave, it is because they are slow, defiant, or disinterested. Through a great deal of communication, the administration understood that Hai's misbehaving necessitated a more challenging curriculum.

APPLICATIONS

▌Application 1

Using an African American or African folklore story, create a setting in your classroom where students learn from each other in multiple ability groupings. After reading, thinking, and writing about the story, students can summarize, analyze, and compare the characters, the plot, and the underlying cultural values that make the characters behave in the way that they do.

▌ Application 2

Learning about the gifts and contributions that different cultural groups make to U.S. society is a way of understanding giftedness. Have students work in groups, with each reading about contributions from a different culture. Each group discusses findings with the total class.

REFLECTIONS

Reflection 1

How does language figure in the way that you perceive students to be gifted and talented?

_____

_____

_____

_____

_____

_____

Reflection 2

What are the social and academic advantages and disadvantages in labeling students as gifted and placing them in accelerated classes?

_____

_____

_____

_____

_____

CHAPTER FIVE

Including Students With Special Needs in the Culturally Responsive Classroom

I recall . . .

In one of my doctoral seminars at UC Santa Barbara, I had a student who was working on a research paper on the placement of students with special needs. When he made a class presentation about his topic, he spoke about being in the first grade, unable to speak English very well. He stood up and tried to tell the teacher that he needed to use the bathroom and she thought that he was disobeying her when she asked him to sit down. He, unfortunately, soiled his pants. Consequently, his inability to speak English got him a placement in a special education class, labeled as a student with "mental retardation." The pain of this misplacement was still evident as he presented his subject to the graduate seminar as tears welled up in his eyes.

For years, before any proactive legislation was enacted to address the special needs of exceptional children, many linguistic and cultural minority children were misplaced in special education classes. Teachers misunderstood their academic requirements and failed to provide an appropriate curriculum. Although much has since been learned and clarified about educating students with disabilities in inclusion classrooms, we have some distance to go. Since the passage of state and federal laws (Wood, 1998), educators who work with culturally diverse students with learning disabilities require adequate preparation to work with students with emotional, behavioral or physical disorders.

Learning disabilities often manifest in behavior problems. Ethnic minority students with disabilities are more likely than white students to be suspended, removed by school personnel, or removed by a hearing officer. Ethnic minority students with disabilities are 67% more likely than whites to be removed on grounds of being dangerous. Up to now, there has been a safeguard in place to provide for due process requirements for young people with a broad category of disabilities in schools. But the U.S. Congress has called for amending the Individuals with Disabilities Education Act (IDEA), which would result in reducing or eliminating critical due process requirements. There are thirteen specific disability categories protected under IDEA (Karten, 2005). These protections are imperative for children of color with disabilities, who are punished at much higher rates than nonminority children (Civil Rights Project, 2003).

The term *special needs* covers the spectrum of difficulties for which students are recommended for special education. Evaluating students for a special placement involves a systematic series of prereferral interventions by a team of educators at the school. The first step is to request a formal observation of the student who is suspected of having a disability. Following the prereferral period, if the student is deemed to have a persistent academic, emotional, or psychological problem, a formal referral process takes place. In this referral step, a team evaluates the student; and depending on the need, a recommendation is made for appropriate placement. Parents are expected to participate in the evaluation conference and give their consent for the student's program. An annual review of the program and the student's progress prevents a student from remaining in an inappropriate placement.

Special needs classrooms focus on the students' potential and the possibility for enhancing their learning through specially designed contexts. However, students from different cultural backgrounds are more likely to be disproportionately placed in special education programs. Educators often assume that their learning difficulties are a result of disabilities rather than linguistic or cultural differences. As a result, they can be mistakenly placed in special education classrooms (Robertson & Kushner, 1994). The Office of Civil Rights and the U.S. Office of Special Education Programs are concerned about disproportionate representation of minority students in special education classes. When students are misclassified and inappropriately labeled, they may not receive the necessary services (Burnette, 1998).

The main goal of special education is to support students with learning disabilities and return them to regular classrooms as soon as possible. Special education placement for students identified as having special needs consists of putting them in either a full-time or part-time special class. Placement in the regular classroom can exist with supplementary instruction, where the student goes to a resource room for part of the day. Including children with special needs in the regular classroom allows all students to win. First, working with their peers increases their sense of belonging. Second, the peers have the opportunity to interact with students who learn differently. As a rule, the most advanced placement for students with special needs is the regular classroom. The student participates in a modified curriculum program. *Inclusion* has been the educational direction taken to provide a more inclusive learning environment for exceptional children.

In an inclusive context, the classroom is designed as a learning setting that permits all children to discover their aptitudes and unique gifts. This involves valuing individual differences and helping students to achieve fully who they are. Theories on multiple intelligences challenge the long-standing beliefs that some children have high intelligence while others are destined for the low-ranks throughout their school career. Our greatest challenge in the classroom is building interpersonal relationships and communication skills between students with special needs and other students.

Sufficient research now shows that it is possible for children with disabilities to work successfully in an inclusion classroom (Karten, 2005). Successful instruction of students with special needs focuses on the students' language use and their interaction with peers.

Teachers in inclusion classrooms require a great deal of support from their school administration as well as the resource specialist staff, and parents. To maintain a successful full-inclusion class, teachers create an explicit social climate that all students understand and practice. Training and support furthers teachers' ability to create safe and productive learning environments.

Historically, students with special needs have been labeled *disabled*, a term that connotes a discrepancy between their potential and achievement. Labeling students as disabled has been a real stigma for many students. That's not to say that they cannot have access to special education programs without it. One issue is that often students who have special needs are considered academically challenged in all academic and social areas. But nothing could be farther from the truth. Just as gifted students are not gifted in all areas of their lives, neither are students with disabilities disabled across the board. They may have untapped talents and intelligence because the classroom environment is too narrowly organized (Diss & Buckley, 2005; Gardner, 1999). Every effort must be made to include children with special needs in an inclusive learning process (Individuals With Disabilities Act, 1990).

The following example describes a second-grade classroom in an inner-city school. Here, the teacher, Mrs. Hansen, describes her approach in creating a learning environment that helps children with special needs to fit into the classroom.

CASE EXAMPLE

Classroom Lesson in an Inclusion Classroom

> **Notice . . .**
>
> *What elements of the lesson assist Robert to complete his work?*

This lesson takes place in late January of the school year. In a language arts group is one of the children diagnosed with Attention Deficit Hyperactivity Disorder (ADHD) and who I'll call Robert. The lesson called for everyone in the group to write about the part of a recently read story they liked best. Some have better writing skill than others. This group works together in an important way. All the students have learned to support each other, and they keep a caring eye on Robert. Students with the disabilities like his often have a problem organizing their time in order to get their work done; their attention spans are shorter. The teacher, Mrs. Hansen, makes only one appearance in the group. But peers encourage each other and Robert eventually gets focused and begins writing.

Carly:	I'm going to write about the way that the boy found his way home after he thought he was lost.
Darin:	(To Robert, who's getting up from his desk) Hey, where are you going?
Robert:	To get a dictionary.
Darin:	OK.
Lily:	How do you spell "horrible"?
Carly:	H-o-r-r-i-b-l-e.
Lily:	Thanks.
	(Darin notices Robert standing by the window looking out. He walks over to Robert to tell him that the dictionaries are on the opposite side of the room.)

(Robert returns to his desk with a dictionary. Minutes into the lesson, the students are thinking and writing.)

Lily: (To Robert, whose eyes are wandering around the room) You'd better get started or you won't finish before we go out to recess.

Robert: I don't care.

Darin: You do too care. You don't want to stay in during recess to finish.

Robert: I don't know what to write.

Carly: It's easy. Just write what part of the story you liked.

(Robert sits quietly looking at his paper.)

Darin: What part did you like?

Robert: I don't know.

(Students shared what they wrote and discussed about the boy finding his way home. They were glad that he could go home and see his mother again.)

(Robert writes the word *The* on his paper and stops.)

(Mrs. Hansen squats down between two students.)

Mrs. Hansen: How are you all doing?

Carly: OK.

Mrs. Hansen: (To Robert) I think that you could use more words to express the part you liked.

Robert: I don't know any more words.

Mrs. Hansen: Tell me what part you liked, and I'll write it down on my pad.

Robert: OK. The boy got home and he was feeling kind of happy.

Mrs. Hansen: All right, I wrote exactly what you said. Now you read it from my pad.

(Robert reads his words which the teacher had written. Then he looked at the teacher as if he was waiting for approval.)

Mrs. Hansen: Good job. Now tell me how long you think it will take you to copy your words onto your paper.

Robert: I don't know.

Mrs. Hansen: What if I set the timer for ten minutes? That will take us to recess time, and I bet you can do it. Here are your words. (She leaves a sheet of paper on his desk.)

Mrs. Hansen continues working with Robert by having him read to her what he has written. After he is finished reading, she asks him if he notices anything, and he realizes that he has left out a word. Mrs. Hansen praises him for recognizing the missing word. He proceeds to insert the word *got*. Mrs. Hansen makes some comments about the lesson.

Mrs. Hansen's Response to the Lesson

Mrs. Hansen reports:

I think all students learn differently, and Robert learns best in short segments of time. Other students can sit and focus on a project for longer periods, but Robert needs his project broken up in smaller chunks. He also needs to know that he's accountable for that what he accomplishes during that period. I try to point out to my class that just as each of them can do one particular thing in a special way, we all learn differently. Some can visualize a particular picture of a house and how a boy looks when I tell a story about a boy and the house in which he lives. In that same way, we all learn differently. I tell them that some can memorize spelling words faster than others, but others can learn more words even if they memorize slower. That doesn't mean that one student is less intelligent than the other one.

Students are very sensitive and understanding about what differences mean. If we're honest with them, we teach them that there isn't anything wrong with learning differently. It's when we don't explain it to them that they begin to tease other kids and treat them like they're dummies. When we talk to them openly, setting clear limits about learning and relating to each other in a caring way—students respond in kind.

Students' Perceptions About the Lesson

Students were interviewed about their working with each other, and here are some of their responses:

- "I don't mind working with others."
- "I like the part where we have to be nice to each other."
- "We have to kinda look after each other, like my parents tell my older brothers at home. They have to kinda look after the younger ones."
- "It's fine. I like helping others. They get to help me, too."
- "My mother says I'm smart and so does the teacher and that makes me feel good."

- "We're supposed to be respectful. My mother tells me to be respectful to the teacher and to be respectful to other kids. I don't mind it."
- "The teacher says that when we help others, we help her teach. That makes me feel smart."

> **Observations:** Teaching students to support other students in group work makes it possible for students with special needs to work alongside others on the same lesson. The teacher's expertise can help students with special needs to manage their time and to develop language skills by interacting with peers.

Comments

Exclusion happens when uniformity and standardization are valued and when learning differences are stigmatized. Inclusion, on the other hand, is a teachable process in any classroom. Accepting attitudes that embrace diverse learning styles diffuse the stigma that students with learning disabilities are less than everyone else because they require special accommodations. Classrooms with more flexible curriculums and learning programs, as well as teachers who teach with a strong perspective of inclusion, build connections among all students.

APPLICATIONS

▌ Application 1

Culturally and linguistically diverse students with learning disabilities often have difficulty understanding a task. A very small way to keep students with special needs from feeling isolated is to ensure that they understand the task by seating them next to another student from the same cultural and linguistic background.

▌ Application 2

Asking students with disabilities questions about whether they comprehend the subject may be culturally inappropriate. Or it may not elicit the response that you would expect. This happens in cases when the students' home culture holds beliefs that it is disrespectful to admit that they do not comprehend. Thus you may want to have students summarize what they just heard.

REFLECTIONS

Reflection 1

In considering the complex needs of students with learning disabilities together with the regular classroom setting, think in general terms about what changes you would need to make to the instructional program.

_____

_____

_____

_____

_____

Reflection 2

How would you present the concept of *inclusion* to parents from a different culture that insists on having their child taught in a separate classroom?

_____

_____

_____

_____

_____

CHAPTER SIX

Culturally Responsive Classroom Management

I recall . . .

It wasn't that sitting forward facing the blackboard was such a new practice for me when I entered Mrs. Brown's second-grade class. I knew that that she wanted us to sit still and not talk to anyone. And although I didn't speak English yet, I knew that my mother was also holding me to being respectful of the teacher's rules. But I did not expect Mrs. Brown to accuse me of copying someone else's paper just because I was picking up my pencil that rolled off the desk. As I leaned down to pick up the pencil, she stepped up to me and said that I was copying from the girl across the aisle from me. My fear and humiliation stole any English words I knew to explain what I was doing—picking up my pencil. Mrs. Brown grabbed my math paper off the top of my desk and tore it up. She handed me a blank page and told me to start again. I felt the tears in my eyes as I faced forward and copied the math problems off the board. As a scared little kid who didn't speak English, I didn't understand how inflexible classroom arrangements could be or that they were set up that way to "help" me learn. That I learned later when I became a teacher. As teachers, we need to understand that the way we arrange the furniture can interfere with learning unless we have the bigger picture in mind and arrange the furniture so that it is an asset to learning without fear and humiliation.

In many classrooms, from east coast to west coast, individual student desks face forward to the blackboard. The teacher stands in front of the class throughout the day and dictates lessons to the students who take notes from the teachers' lessons written on the board. At a designated time, the teacher asks the students to recall information and answer questions. Students' hands rise and the teacher selectively calls on them or may choose to call on the students who do not raise their hands. Students typically have to secure permission to leave their seats to travel to another part of the classroom or to the restroom. The type of interaction that usually prevails in this classroom model is that the teacher questions and the students answer. Peer verbal interaction is not encouraged and most often disallowed. Routinely, this form of class arrangement fosters individual competitiveness that is designed to test student's knowledge of a specific body of information.

Yet it has been established that when students work collectively in groups, they interact more fully, increasing opportunities for learning. This form of pedagogy has shown marked improvement in reaching students because it establishes continuity between their homes and the school.

Continuity is necessary —and so is discontinuity. When students experience discontinuity between their home and school languages, values or expectations, it may interfere with their learning. However, the school is also responsible for teaching students different kinds of experiences, and how that is accomplished is what makes it succeed or fail. In this chapter, we see how Mrs. Jones determines her students' needs and decides to break with the school's program to provide her students a culturally responsive classroom.

Mrs. Jones, a second-grade teacher, helps us to see that there is more to teaching than is arranging the furniture. On the face of it, Mrs. Jones's approach to teaching may seem like a throw back to the 1950s. And to some extent, it is. However, she reminds us that cultural continuity and understanding the cultural arrangement of the classroom furniture can come in different forms. And diversity of approach among teachers is justified, especially if the results are effective as those of Mrs. Jones.

CASE EXAMPLE

Notice . . .

What convinces Mrs. Jones that her teaching approach is effective?

A middle-sized, urban community that often finds itself in the news headlines for violence on the streets is also home to some very dedicated classroom teachers. In one particular classroom, Mrs. Jones has taught second grade for seven years. Prior to that, she taught in Missouri. Observing her room, one could easily believe that it's neat rows facing forward and the quiet environment is the most ideal setting for learning. After all, the students behaved well, the parents didn't complain, and the teacher received excellent evaluations from the principal. Most notably, students achieved well in their academic subjects.

Mrs. Jones's classroom was ethnically mixed, composed of 70% African American, 20% Latino, and 10% European American students. Everyone involved with this classroom—the teacher, the students, and the parents—described it as a good class. Parents did not complain about the class because, as one of them put it, "If she can control those kids, there's no reason to complain." Another parent commented on the fact that her son finally memorized his multiplication tables because Mrs. Jones drilled them until they learned them. Mrs. Jones talks about her class and explains her reason for not changing the way she has taught since she began teaching:

Mrs. Jones

Mrs. Jones moved west from Missouri, where she and her husband both taught. He was a high school teacher and she, an elementary school teacher. In her words,

> We like living in the same communities that we teach in because we get to know the families. I run into them in church or at the store. This helps me when I have to discipline the students. They know that I know where they live and that I talk to their parents away from school. I also know that most of the children in this community are from working-class families that may not support their schoolwork. They require a structure in which they can work that helps them to be still, quiet, and orderly. On the streets and in many of their homes, there's a lot of loud noise and shouting. I don't think those are environments conducive for learning. Many of these children work hard on their schoolwork even in those conditions. But I believe that they can be provided something different.

Mrs. Jones prefers teaching second grade because the children are becoming more independent in their reading and writing. She prefers not to offer students many choices:

> Today students are expected to have too many choices about what to learn, how they want to learn, and how they feel about it. I think all that does is let the teachers off the hook. We're supposed to make the decisions because that's what we're paid to do. We're supposed to help the students learn what is important. They don't know what's valuable. We do. That's our job.

Mrs. Jones's approach to teaching, however, was a source of some consternation for Mr. Kenny, the school principal. He had different expectations for the teaching staff. He wanted teachers to conform to a uniform school curriculum, which required a variety of instructional methodologies.

Mrs. Jones's Classroom

On the wall next to the door, students' papers with 100% correct spelling lists were displayed in neat rows, one after the next. Below the spelling lists were compositions graded A and A- all neatly lined up from one end of the board to the other. Together, they covered the entire bulletin board under the heading, "Good Work!" Thirty-two individual desks faced toward the front of the class. Mrs. Jones's desk sat in the back of the room next to the door. Her desk, too, faced forward where she could watch the backs of the students' heads.

Math Lesson

Mrs. Jones: Please bring up your completed worksheets and place them in this box. (She points to the box in front of her.)

(Students hand their papers forward to the person in front until they all reach the first person in front.)

Jerome: (Raises his hand) I couldn't finish all of my homework because I didn't understand it all. But I turned in what I did finish.

Mrs. Jones: Then you'll be graded accordingly. And you have to stay after school so I can work with you on that.

Charlene: (Raises hand) I didn't understand it all either, Mrs. Jones. My mother tried to help me, but I still didn't get it.

Mrs. Jones: Then we've better go through it together again in class. You and everyone who didn't turn in their homework stay after school, and we'll work on it together.

Still on the math lesson, Mrs. Jones turned toward the board. "Please pay attention to how you do these problems. First, begin by multiplying with the ones unit as if it was the only number you have to use. Then, once you're done that and written down the product, begin to multiply with the number in the tens place. Remember to list the product one place to the left from your last product. I've done this one for you on the board. Now let's do one together." Mrs. Jones then asked everyone to call out the directions and she would place the numbers wherever they indicated.

Following the collective problem solving, Mrs. Jones asked for volunteers to come to the board to solve the other multiplication problems. She called on one student at a time. Each went up to the board and solved the problem with minimal prompting from the teacher. While students went up to work on the board, Mrs. Jones stood partway toward the back of the room and watched other students, calling on individuals to pay attention when their eyes strayed from the board.

When all of the problems on the board were solved, Mrs. Jones handed out a sheet with rows of similar problems for them to solve independently at their desks. Mrs. Jones told the students, "I know that every one of you can get every one of these problems correct."

Mrs. Jones walked up and down the rows of students monitoring them as they completed the worksheet she gave them. One student stopped her to ask a question and as she stopped to answer, two students in the back of the room leaned toward each other, whispering. One of the students pointed to his paper and the other one looked on his. At that moment, they heard the teacher's voice, "Everyone, do your own work!" Both boys sat back in their seats and returned to writing on their respective papers. Two other people held up their hands and the teacher went to answer their questions. Thirty minutes after Mrs. Jones began the assignment, she asked the students to pass their papers forward.

Mrs. Jones called out to the class, "All right, get yourselves ready for recess." When the bell rang, she dismissed them one row at a time.

But for Mrs. Jones and two students, part of the recess was spent in her explaining how to solve the math problem. As Mrs. Jones was dismissing the students, she pointed to Alex and David to sit at the table by the board. She followed them to the table and asked Alex to write the problem, 23 multiplied by 11. Mrs. Jones asked David to multiply the 1×3, then 1×2. Alex then said he knew how to do the next step. He took the chalk and wrote the answer, but it was in the ones place rather than in the tens place. Mrs. Jones reminded them that the tens place was one space to the left. He wrote it down correctly; then Mrs. Jones prompted them about what the last step was. "You have to add all of the numbers," said Alex. "Go ahead and do it," instructed Mrs. Jones. When they finished, Mrs. Jones then told them, "That's the way you do the rest of the problems on your sheet. Now go out and use the restroom before the bell rings."

Fitting in With the School Plan

Mr. Kenny marveled at how Mrs. Jones continued to fit in, with a staff that constantly underwent changes and with new programs to address the school's academic challenges:

It's not as though I haven't tried to get her to change and try new ways of teaching. When I first arrived, it was my mission to change her until I realized what she had going for her was so in line with what we all wanted for the students. The difference was that we couldn't pull off what she does so well. And the reason it works for her and could never work for other teachers here is that it's a part of who she is, what she believes, and how she lives her life. She believes that the students will learn because it's up to her to make it happen, even when some of the parents don't support the students like she expects. The other thing about her classroom is that she does work along with the school's plan. She uses the same curriculum that we use for all the subjects, except that she doesn't have students work in a variety of settings. Most of our curriculum recommends that we use interactive-type activities.

> **Observations:** Mrs. Jones's respect and high expectation for her students validates their potential. She demonstrates the positive aspects of cultural discontinuity that builds a supportive learning environment for her students. In effect, she provides a strong learning setting by emphasizing quiet and orderliness, allowing them to concentrate and work in an orderly fashion.

Comments

No single approach to classroom arrangement guarantees learning; what's crucial is that teachers like Mrs. Jones arrange their classrooms to support student learning in every way possible. And the students respond. Mrs. Jones's pedagogy is governed by her knowledge of the community, her knowledge of the students' home life, and knowledge of their academic abilities. Accordingly, she designed a classroom setting responsive to their needs. How teachers organize their classrooms sets the expectations for their students' learning. Mrs. Jones clearly had an authoritarian arrangement in her classroom, and she expected a great deal from the students. Yet it was a supportive setting, as demonstrated by the time that she was willing to give them.

Although we might think that the setup depicted Mrs. Jones as a sole authority, this was not just a case of her exerting her power. She lived in the community, communicated with her students' families, and was familiar with their social and emotional requisites. Mrs. Jones's classroom arrangement succeeded because it was congruent with her knowledge of the community. She held high expectations for her students. She expected the students to work independently and do their own work. In this setting,

Mrs. Jones's teaching tradition worked for her students because they rose to her expectations and performed accordingly.

In the teacher education literature, the example of Mrs. Jones's class could be mistaken for an "outdated," "rigid," or "monolithic" approach to teaching. However, Mrs. Jones's intentions and her expectations for the students, as well as her connection to the community, are culturally consistent with her pedagogy. Her techniques says, "I expect you to perform to the highest potential, and I'll support you in doing so."

APPLICATIONS

Application 1

Teacher-parent meetings are good opportunities to learn about family values and practices. Ask specific open-ended questions to parents, such as the following: "Tell me about your family mealtimes together." "How do you discipline your child at home?" "What things are causes for disciplining your child?" "What would be the most successful thing your child could do in a single day?" Get parents to open up about their expectations for their children and how they get them to succeed at being a child learner.

Application 2

Learning about your students' home culture and using the information to their advantage in the classroom can be accomplished by having students keep personal journals.

REFLECTIONS

Reflection 1

Consider how you liked classroom learning when you were in school. What type of classroom arrangement did you prefer? What role did classroom seating play in your classroom learning when you were in school?

_____

_____

_____

_____

_____

Reflection 2

Supposing you were an administrator in the school where Mrs. Jones taught, how would you have her share her understanding of the community's culture with other teachers in the school?

_____

_____

_____

_____

_____

CHAPTER SEVEN

Supporting Children's Cultural Adjustment

I recall . . .

Sometimes my classroom peers teased me about not speaking English and not understanding what went on in the classroom. When I would tell my mother what the kids told me, she would just say that they didn't understand and that I should be proud that I speak another language and that I was learning English, which made her very proud of me.

In memory, however, I returned to my former school days in Mexico. If I closed my eyes, I could still smell the musty old school building and hear my friends' lively voices singing *naranja dulce* and other popular circle games and jingles. The Spanish alphabet letters pinned neatly in the front of the classroom above the blackboard formed a background behind the young teacher, whose warm smile greeted us every day. By the second grade in my Mexican school, I was reading history books. I missed my days in Mexico, where the language and books were familiar and where my friends understood me. I was a star student before I immigrated legally with my family to the United States. Now I had to repeat the second grade because I didn't speak English, something that just didn't happen fast enough for me. Until I could do that, I was going to have to be grateful for the fun memories of a place I called home.

E ven before new students from diverse cultural groups step foot in your classroom, they face many new classmates who have many questions: Where are you from? Do you speak English? What country did you live in? What school did you go to? What was your school like? Do you have brothers or sisters? Whether the arriving students are from a community nearby or from a country across the world, they feel new. Students adjust culturally to new locations depending on way that the receiving school and community takes care to integrate them into the new setting and their connection to their previous communities. Cultural identity matters to students as they form new relationships to other students from different cultural groups.

It is known that the stronger students feel about their cultural identity, the better their academic work will be (Mahiri, 2004; Mohatt & Erickson, 1982; Ogbu, 1982; Sadowski, 2003; Spindler, 1977, 1982). Schools can either support students' cultural adjustment: They can acknowledge and continue the students' strong sense of cultural identity and assist them in adjusting to their new community with a sense of integrity. The opposite is also possible. If students face rejection and lack of appreciation, cultural conflicts are likely to ensue. How students from different cultural groups adjust to their respective communities involves their perceptions about themselves and their lives as well as of their new setting. In the classroom, culturally different students can be engaged through reading, writing, and sharing about their connection to their home countries, their friends, and their families.

In this chapter, I describe some aspects of the lives of Russian refugee students in a middle-sized urban community, to better understand how that adjustment takes place. I describe their cultural setting in their community and out of school, including their family values that inform their sense of identity. The question of cultural identity is a factor in learning because students want connection with all three: family, teachers, and peers. It's central in making sense of their status within those cultural communities. Students wrestle with discovering who they are in their new setting by recalling who they were in their former homeland. The students' day-to-day interactions with their cultural history, their institutional community support from organizations such as churches, and the way teachers utilize this wealth of information and knowledge which students bring to school all shape their cultural adjustment.

The small urban community of Yolo, California, became home to a sizable Russian refugee group in the 1990s, when a large immigration took place. The city of Yolo invited the Russian families to live there, having become home to several earlier similar influxes. Russian immigrant arrivals in Yolo proceeded in four major phases: (1) a pre-1917 settlement, (2) an immigration between 1917–1945, (3) a post-World War II settlement, and (4) a post-Soviet Union immigration in the 1980s and 1990s (Bronfenbrenner, 1973; Johnson, 1981). Many Russians immigrating in the early 1900s intermarried, changed their names, and made every effort to "melt in." A community leader quoted his mother, who had arrived in the second phase, "Thank God, we don't look different. Even though our culture is quite different, we can melt into the general mainstream." This group was also well educated and wealthy. It resided in or around well-established Russian neighborhoods existing in the surrounding areas.

A broad range of housing options were available in Yolo for new arrivals. There were numerous apartment developments, there were trailer parks, and motels provided rentals at weekly rates. A wide range of lower housing prices was available throughout the city. Yolo had six elementary schools, one middle school, and two high schools that constituted the Yolo School District. Four parochial schools also served the area; two elementary and two high schools. The public schools had large, ethnically diverse populations. The largest group other than European Americans was Latino, followed by Russian refugees, Hmong Americans, and Mien Americans. A few Arabic, Hindi, Samoan, Laotian, Khmer, and Punjabi students also attended those schools.

The dynamic of cultural adjustment manifesting itself in the schools was of particular interest to local educators. Teachers, family members, and community leaders contributed to our understanding of cultural identity in the classroom. Russian community leaders, including the directors of social service agencies; ministers in the Baptist, Pentecostal, and Russian Orthodox churches; Head Start family specialists; as well as Russian translators for young students and families, played a dominant role in the students' cultural adjustment to their new community. An aspect of the families' social and cultural adjustment involved knowledge and appreciation of their family lives in the former homelands—Russia, Ukraine, Estonia, and Latvia.

CASE EXAMPLE

Russian Families

About 700 Russians immigrated during 1989, and many others continued to arrive over the next five years to be reunited with their families. About sixty families arrived in one week during the height of this period. Family size varied, depending on who had been

> *Notice . . .*
>
> *What cultural expectations from parents did Russian students take to school?*

able to obtain passports. Families tended to be large, however, because their Pentecostal religion encouraged reliance on divine providence where having children is concerned, and many of these families had nine, ten, or eleven children.

The Russian parents in this recent cohort of refugees were under forty years of age and had children whose ages ranged from a few months old to twenty years. Most adults had completed the equivalent of a high school education in their former homelands and had been employed as skilled workers, including truck drivers, nonmigratory agricultural workers, restaurant cooks, and teachers in the lower grades; these last had received some low-level English training. When queried about aspirations for their children, Russian parents expressed a desire to have them become successful Americans. This desire was usually qualified with the additional goal that their children maintain their Russian culture, including the language, religion, and important customs.

Most Russian adults attended daily English classes, and their employability improved as a result of having more English skills. Their responses to having this time to study varied, since some believed that it was divine providence that allowed them this opportunity as well as welfare assistance. Some felt frustrated that they were studying instead of working. Others felt frustrated by not being able to work because of their limited English ability and the depressed job market.

For example, the Scalzi household had thirteen children, but only Mr. Scalzi was able to work, since Mrs. Scalzi was not well. Mr. Scalzi was forty-five years old and did not speak English; his only skill was his ability to drive a bus. Part-time jobs for which most adults were qualified paid minimum wages and had no provisions for health coverage. Thus, these refugee families unquestionably were dependent on welfare. This assistance provided families with the equivalent of twice the minimum wage and health provisions for the family. This health coverage assistance seemed invaluable to most families, given their needs.

Russian parents emphasized religious values as a way of imposing control over their children. Close affiliation with the Baptist and Pentecostal churches was more than a religious practice. Church communities acted as extended families, offering adult English lessons, translations, and other information, as well as family counseling for parents who have difficulty with adolescent children.

Russian students who immigrated as adolescents had a difficult time adjusting to their new school and community. Although the parents valued education, they criticized the U.S. schooling system for being too easy in comparison with education in the former Soviet Union. In particular, they said that students complained about the boring classes, which they believed to be inferior. While parents understood their children's dilemma, their concern was more about their loss of control, and the schools failed to enforce familial authority.

In Russia, students did not have the luxury of open campuses and freedom to come and go as they pleased: Some students abused some of their privileges here. Between their feelings of boredom and the liberty accorded them, many Russian students found it easier to stay out of school and drive around, smoking and imbibing alcohol. When parents were contacted by the schools, their response was that it was the school's problem and one that would never have occurred in Russia: There, the students would have spent two weeks in a work camp, after which, they say, the discipline problem would have disappeared.

Parents sometimes resorted to calling upon the church pastor to talk with the children and pray for them, in the case of discipline problems. They trusted their counsel. Children were encouraged to return to correct behavior in the name of the Lord and to obey their parents. Usually, counseling sessions with the families about their adolescents' behavior were minimally effective. Students were simply encouraged to find other, more wholesome outlets, such as church activities, to express their freedom. Unfortunately, Yolo offered little outside of school and church activities for students. There was a movie theater and a video store in town; beyond that, students had to travel to other communities for recreation.

Social Support for Russian Families

There was an unusual link between Russia and Yolo—a cultural translator named Mr. Ovodov who was one of the immigrants who came to Yolo in 1950. He organized an evangelistic radio program that was transmitted to the Philippines as well as to Turkey and the Soviet Union. This program converted many people in the Soviet Union. The more recent Russian immigrants tell about persecution in the former Soviet Union, including having their homes bugged with listening devices and of being accused spying for the American government. They were often detained at the local police headquarters or KGB offices for questioning. Many of their children were also denied higher educational opportunities because of their religious affiliations and refusal to be in the Communist Party.

Mr. Ovodov became a much respected community leader because he was also an English teacher who had studied in an American university after arriving in Yolo as a teenager. Beginning in the mid-1980s, Mr. Ovodov organized efforts to help bring Russian families from the Pentecostal and Baptist faiths into Yolo. He met with real estate business people in the community as well as with representatives of the health clinic and the Christian Center. Mr. Ovodov proposed bringing other Russian families as refugees and to provide them community services and support from the time they arrived by plane to the time they sent their children to school—services that would continue throughout their stay in Yolo. He established powerful connections with Russians who were long-standing citizens in Yolo as well as with social service agencies. He laid the groundwork with community agencies and made appointments with social service centers prior to the arrival of Russian families. In this way, Russians who immigrated had the advantage of knowing the type of services available to them and how to access them.

Prominent Russians who were long-time residents in Yolo sometimes hesitated in assisting the recent refugees who had lived under communism. However, there still seemed to be a strong affirmative response to the call for translators in the schools and volunteers to fill out forms in the social service agencies and to find housing for these incoming refugees. This ethnic network greatly eased the process for the newcomers.

In Yolo, the Russian Orthodox, Baptist, and Pentecostal churches held services in Russian as well as in English. The social integration of earlier arrivals and the political power of the Russian community presented a strong base for the refugee group.

Yolo schools organized a variety of programs in their efforts to deal with culturally and linguistically diverse students. Although the most prevalent theoretical orientations seemed to be those of cultural deficit or continuity-discontinuity, some teachers attempted to work with innovative pedagogical notions of educating students from diverse cultural backgrounds.

Differences of Students and Parents

Russian students typically raised questions in class and were called on by teachers to answer questions, while students from other groups waited to be called on by teachers before raising any questions.

A major difference between the Russians and the other cultural groups was the assertive way in which Russian parents approached classroom teachers to inquire about their children's academic progress. Russian parents approached the teachers, although they did not speak English very fluently. The children translated for them as they inquired about homework or progress in class. This was in comparison with other parents who usually waited for their children at the gate outside.

What Stories Tell

Although school programs seemed to have limited results in promoting multicultural understanding between students in Yolo, two teachers in this study surfaced as exceptional educators, distinguished by their use of literacy and emphasis on a more comprehensive cultural program in their respective classrooms. These exemplary teaching practices were isolated in their respective settings, but nonetheless, demonstrated the importance of allowing student voices to emerge, through stories. As conceived by these two teachers, student stories had great merit because they departed from the usual ways of constructing stories and were based on a comprehensive conception of using curriculum for the purpose of enhancing the self, family, and community. Although Ms. Suarez and Ms. Diaz did not work together, their approaches to teaching resembled one another in that they created a challenging learning environment in the classroom which extended into students' families and community.

Ms. Suarez taught sixth grade but also taught English as a second language to a group of Russian students. She taught herself to speak Russian by offering Russian families English lessons and spending a great deal of time in the Russian community. Families befriended her and invited her to events that further informed her understanding and the classroom curriculum.

In her classroom, family histories and experiences in Yolo were explored through stories that students wrote and shared with each other. At the beginning of the school year, students were assigned to write a story *with their parents*. It could be one told to them by their parents about their life in their former homeland, about the immigration experience, or one of the students' favorite stories. The children and their parents' disparate English skills made this assignment difficult, but it was an important one. The parents were expected to write the story in their first language, but if they couldn't, the children were instructed to bring the story in some other form—either on audiotape or written in English.

The teacher then assisted each of the students in translating their stories into English. Usually, the teacher recruited volunteer translators to help in the process. Once the stories were in written English, the teacher duplicated them and bound them, and they became reading texts for the class. Every student shared his or her story orally as they read it from their texts. A third-grade Russian student, Elina, wrote this story, which was told to her by her mother:

> When my mom was a little girl, she remembers when a lot of people came in her village. These people acted very happy and friendly. They were walking everywhere. My mom remembers how these people invited many people to visit them and offered them gold. The people at first did not trust the friendly strangers, but they started to buy gold for very little money. Mother remembers how her parents bought gold too. Soon the friendly strangers left the village [text unedited].

Ms. Suarez also utilized storytelling to build understanding between the children, enabling them to learn about each other's histories and experiences of adjustment. Maintaining ties between the children and their parents was a goal in the process, since Ms. Suarez believed that the students were going through an emotional rupture from their families and cultures. Consequently, she used stories to foster intergenerational communication between parents and students. They began an open dialogue in the classroom around issues that were germane to the students' emotional adjustment. Nila's story illustrates her ambivalence in coming to the United States:

> I came to the United States from Russia because of religion. Life was nice there. There were many birds singing in the morning and pretty flowers and forests. We could pick different kinds of berries. We were happy except for one thing. The government didn't like Christians. When people got together to pray, and the police saw them, they had to pay a lot of money, and the pastor had to go to jail for three or four years. I know a man who was in jail for twenty years because he told a lot of people about God.
>
> In school in Russia, they picked a student to act like the boss. They picked an A+ student who never said bad words. Once they picked me. It was fun. I was surprised when I came to school here that girls were wearing earrings and makeup and jeans. They weren't wearing uniforms. I thought I'd still have to wear one, and I hate uniforms!
>
> In Russia, everyone hated the Christians, but here the students hate the Russians. It is crazy because the Bible says that all people are really the same. We just speak different languages because when he was making Israel, God made the Tower of Babel and separated the languages [edited by the teacher].

This English class was a busy one, where Ms. Suarez had several parents assisting students at any given time. Here, as in Ms. Diaz's class, students communicated through stories and shared their feelings with their parents as they reconstructed their life experiences to share with their classmates. Adult-child interactions revealed the areas of interest in the families.

The question of school adjustment for these ethnic and linguistically different students merits examination beyond the classroom curriculum. Consider the complex relationships which students had outside of the school, including the social and political history of the groups in Yolo as well as the family lives and their struggle to obtain the necessary resources to survive. As we've seen, some teachers harnessed the students' rich cultural experiences to assist them in their emotional adjustment. They helped students build a link between the school and the community.

> **Observations:** The teachers' use of personal student narratives provided students with opportunities to appreciate and connect their history and culture to their new circumstances.

Comments

What determines whether students are adjusting successfully to a new school or community? The Russian refugee example revealed that the students learned English when they fit in with the school community without any major disruption. The parents connected with the school personnel. And in turn, teachers responded to the students' needs in their curriculum by allowing them to share their stories in writing. The Russian students helped us to understand their social and cultural adjustment when the classroom curriculum was organized to assist them in the process (Delgado-Gaitan & Trueba, 1991; Hall, 1990; Trueba, 1989).

In Yolo, Russian families orchestrated their social and cultural context as they made meaning of their daily practices to obtain their desired resources. And the school was one principal avenue. Curricular techniques, such as story sharing, can help us to understand how cultural conflicts affect students' thinking. For fuller understanding, it's equally important to consider the people's historical, cultural, political, and socioeconomic conditions. Culturally responsive instruction takes into account the students' knowledge of their community, family histories, and personal connection to their new community. Ms. Suarez and Ms. Diaz's pedagogy appreciated the students' voices and emotional development.

The two teachers recognized the heterogeneity of the community and appreciated the students' interaction with it in their attempts to make learning meaningful and facilitate the students' ability to access the high quality of education available to students of the dominant group.

APPLICATIONS

Application 1

Design a lesson in any subject matter that allows all students to share their experiences of connecting with someone from a different culture, in their classroom, school, or community.

▌Application 2

Introducing music, dance, and food from a different culture is fine, but make it meaningful. For example, instead of students just watching and then learning a dance, have them interview the dancers or musicians about the stories behind their performances. Then link the students' writing about the artists to books about people in the arts.

REFLECTIONS

Reflection 1

Helping students from other backgrounds succeed in a new culture is partly the school's responsibility. Think about how you can get students from a different culture to share their experiences of living in a new community.

_____

_____

_____

_____

_____

Reflection 2

Suppose you are a student who moved to a new location and culture where you had to speak a new language. What would you want to learn about in class as quickly as possible if you had no friends at home to teach you?

_____

_____

_____

_____

_____

CHAPTER EIGHT

Connecting Home and School

> **I recall . . .**
>
> Remember the days of classroom mothers? Long before there was research on parent involvement, I was convinced that learning was a family and school partnership. Both of my parents spoke limited English, and neither had formal schooling in Mexico. But that didn't stop my mother from showing up with armloads of cupcakes for our classroom on Fridays when she was room mother. Although she didn't speak much English when we immigrated, she was a strong and visible influence in my life both in school and at home. It mattered to me that my mother held high expectations for me and my sisters to succeed in school and that she got involved in whatever way she could, because I knew that I had to try my best. She wanted to hear good reports about me from my teachers.

Without question, the family and the school are the two institutions that most influence students' development and learning. Students' academic performances improve through effective communication between parents and teachers throughout the students' schooling (Epstein et al., 2002). The usefulness of home and school connections depends largely on how culturally continuous or discontinuous they are. However, home-school relationships cannot be characterized simply as continuous or discontinuous. Instead, an effective classroom setting incorporates both the students' and the mainstream classroom culture.

Cultural continuity between home and school occurs through shared cultural beliefs and expectations. Such continuity is most evident in communities where parents have attended schools similar to those that their children now attend. In such cases, parents are more likely to recognize the importance of staying informed about their children's schooling. They are familiar with the way the school operates. They know the personnel in charge of the various functions of the school and the appropriate language necessary to make their concerns known. Knowing this, parents establish ongoing contact with teachers and other school personnel.

On the other hand, cultural discontinuity occurs in various ways when parents and teachers do not explicitly share values, beliefs, or practices. For example, if teachers are permissive in disciplining students in the classroom while parents expect stricter disciplining, this discontinuity may create problems. When students experience learning problems, a strong dialogue between parents and teachers can uncover underlying beliefs and practices that may shed light on the immediate concern. Robins, Lindsey, Lindsey, and Terrell (2002) suggest that when learners experience difficulties, "It is not the learners' cultural behaviors and patterns that are suspect, but rather, it is this instructor's behavior that must change and adapt to meet their needs for learning" (p. 83).

PARENT AND TEACHER PARTNERSHIPS

The culture of most schools is more congruent with families whose cultural and socioeconomic backgrounds are mainstream, European American, and middle class. This is evident in the numbers of European American parents who traditionally participate in the school's organized activities, as opposed to those parents from culturally diverse, often working-class families. Their absence in school activities has been interpreted as indifference about their children's schooling. However, vast research shows that culturally different parents do care about their children's school performance. The problem is that they lack the cultural knowledge to participate actively. The difficulty of parental access to schools also precludes the schools' connection with families and communities. This points to the conclusion that informed parents are likely to be the most involved in their children's education. To participate actively in their children's schooling, parents have to learn how the school operates, including the language needed, the personnel in charge, and the protocol to reach teachers and administrators. All parents can learn how to use the process and build healthy parent-teacher relationships.

Parent-teacher partnerships can be, conventional or unconventional. Conventional practices, such as parent-teacher conferences and open house evenings, have historically been organized by schools to report on students' progress. These parent-teacher activities assume that parents know how to stay involved in the children's education day to day. The school typically designs these conventional activities without parental input. PTAs and some school site councils fit in this category, given the nature of the decision-making groups that operate in a mainstream cultural way. Schools that receive federal and state funding require parents to participate in the decision making of the program.

The driving assumption of parent-school partnerships is that the family, school, and community are interrelated because children learn and act in all those places according to their family values and beliefs. Whether parents believe it or not, they know information about how their children learn, such as their interests and their abilities. Such information is essential to the success of classroom curriculum. The purpose of parent-teacher partnerships lies beyond an increase in test scores. Parents have to deal with children's schooling long past preschool and early grades. After the third grade, students from linguistic and culturally diverse groups are at a higher academic risk if their parents fear the schools and cannot understand their children's homework. To enlist this crucial parental involvement, schools must develop culturally responsive, systematic approaches to working with parents.

Parents and teachers hold a great deal of power regarding children's learning. How they utilize their power together is central to building effective parent involvement partnerships. Where some parent-teacher groups may focus on fundraising or other issues that indirectly deal with children, more effective groups focus on the children and the day-to-day activities related to their education. One such organization is the Latino Parent Committee (LPC), originally organized by a group of Latino parents to support and inform each other about the schools, which mobilized more involvement in their children's education. The LPC parents invited school district personnel to attend their meetings. They also extended the invitation to teachers. A school district director always attended district-level LPC meetings, but teachers attended less frequently. And that was just fine with the parents. They believed that the teachers worked very hard in the classrooms. Latino parents worked closely with the teachers anyway, and both shared a common interest—the children. With children as the central focus of the organization, the parents wanted to be fully informed and to cooperate with the schools to support their children's learning.

Parents and teachers collaborated through the school-site LPC meetings. Teachers made presentations to parents at meetings about their classroom curriculum in Spanish. Parents were able to ask questions about the presentation and to pose other questions about their children's schooling. In that way, teachers and parents shared knowledge with one another.

Here's what Mr. Sanders, the district director, had to say about LPC:

What makes LPC different from other standard parent groups is that they organized it on their own. We didn't do it. And that gives them the power to conduct it in the way that is important to them and which will accomplish their specified goals and objectives. It's not static. It changes as needed. It's organized to teach parents about children's day-to-day learning practices.

At a parent-teacher meeting which Latino parents organized in a primary school, Mrs. Calvo, a second-grade teacher, volunteered to make a presentation about the math program in her classroom. About twenty parents attended the evening meeting held at the library. Her presentation lasted about a half hour. She showed and described the math textbook that she used in her class. She also explained how she used supplementary materials to assist children in learning math concepts. She also suggested ways that parents could assist their children at home. The following excerpts are from the teacher-parent interaction. The meeting was all in Spanish, and here it is translated to English. Not all of the parents who attended spoke during the dialogue.

Mrs. Calvo: One of the most successful parts of the math program is what I call a two-buddy system. I pair-up the children to assist each other when they're working on a specific assignment. With the buddy system, students have one person to whom they can turn to assist them if they have questions until I can get to them. If their first buddy can't help them, they have permission to go to a second person for help.

Mrs. Salas: Is that what people call *cooperative learning*?

Mrs. Calvo: Not exactly. Cooperative learning is when a group of students solve a problem together. In the buddy system they're each responsible for their own work, but they can talk about it with each other or someone else if they need.

Mrs. Mora: Doesn't this mean that they can copy from each other?

Mrs. Calvo: I teach them how to ask for help and how to give help without copying. They know the difference and because they trust that someone is there to help them, they're not as tempted to want to copy from someone. The idea is for them to learn how to find the necessary help. That's a skill which we often don't teach until high school, when they write reports. They need to feel confident to ask for help when they don't know how to work out a problem.

Mr. Rico:	What if the student they're asking gives them a wrong answer?
Mrs. Calvo:	I review the work with each student, and we also do it together as a group.
Mrs. Garcia:	Do you count right and wrong answers? I mean, I don't want my child to get the wrong answer because another student gave them wrong information on how to work out a problem.
Mrs. Calvo:	I understand your concern, but part of the way that I teach students to help each other actually helps them in the thinking process. You see, when you have to explain to someone how to solve a problem, you get to learn it even better. So it's good for the person giving assistance and for the student receiving it. I tell them that the thinking behind the answer—how they arrived at their answer—is just as important as the answer—maybe more so.
Mrs. Honda:	What you're saying is that the buddy system helps them to talk about the problem and try to solve it with someone. And that kind of talking together is beneficial for their learning.
Mrs. Calvo:	Exactly.
Mr. Alvarez:	I think what you're doing is wonderful because that's what I teach my children to do at home—to help each other.
Mrs. Calvo:	That's the point. They don't always learn more by doing it alone. In real life, like you're saying that you teach your children at home, we rely on each other for help. I teach them to explain the assignment to someone else. In that way, they use language and get to explain the process to someone else.
Mrs. Salas:	Mrs. Calvo, what's the best way that we can help our children at home with math? I know my child has a hard time with it even when I help him.
Mrs. Calvo:	A major thing to do at home is to help them know how they arrived at their answer. You can use beans, fruit, chairs, whatever works to get them to concretely and physically see the problem that they have to solve and to think about the steps that are involved in order to solve it.

Questions and comments on the part of parents show a willingness to listen to each other and respect the points of view of the people present. As I write this, the LPC continues to meet monthly. Their topics vary, and together they learn and solve problems to better serve their children.

Communication between parents and teachers is critical in supporting student success in schooling. By successes, I do not necessarily mean only grades or standardized test scores. Sometimes success occurs in different ways, such as enabling a student to receive proper placement in a special-needs or an accelerated program. Well-established home-school connections provide a vehicle for the two institutions to come together whenever it's necessary. Without these connections in place, schools and families may not reach out to each other.

Differences in the way that families and schools relate depend on the socioeconomic characteristics of the community, its social and historic community relations with schools, and the cultural experience of families (Lareau & Shumar, 1996). Stereotypical views about families who live in low socioeconomic conditions hold that such parents do not care about their children's education. Nothing could be farther from the truth. If working-class families are less visible in the schools, we cannot assume that they are less caring than middle-class parents. Frequent misperceptions about working-class parents or parents from different ethnic groups also create stereotypes. The belief is that parents who speak a language other than English don't help their children with their schoolwork. Such judgments only interfere with the possibilities for them to learn how to communicate with their school to help their children. For example, working-class parents have often experienced a great deal of failure in their backgrounds, which may inhibit their contact with their children's school. This may be hard for teachers to understand, much less to attempt to engage these parents in school activities. However, research has shown that these parents are not resisting contact with the school. Rather, they fear the school setting because they are unfamiliar with it. Parents and teachers oftentimes hold stereotypes about each other when there hasn't been much meaningful contact between the families and the school. But thinking in stereotypical ways obscures the reality of people's real experience. Stereotypes that teachers hold about parents, and vice versa, disadvantage the students' opportunities for support. But through parent education, families can learn to assist their children and advocate for them (Delgado Gaitan, 2004; Epstein & Sanders, 2002).

The connections between schools and families are valuable to the extent that they build trusting relationships. The important thing is to maintain open and flexible ways to relate to each other.

PARENT INVOLVEMENT

Parent involvement has as many different meanings as there are school districts. Unquestionably, parents are an integral part of children's schooling through the guidance they exercise at home. Parent involvement is sometimes confused with parent education, but there are specific

Figure 8.1

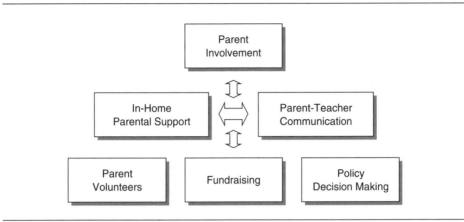

differences. Although parent education is part of the larger umbrella of parent involvement, I use five general areas to define parent involvement: working with the children in the home, parent-teacher communication, classroom volunteering, fundraising, and policy making. See Figure 8.1.

In the Home. At home, parents perform endless tasks that impact children's learning. Parents can support their children in visible and invisible ways. Cultural activities in the home guide children's lives and prepare them physically, emotionally, and psychologically. Parents set guidelines and expectations for their children's behavior in the home and at school. Those who are familiar with the school's expectations can design activities that stimulate children's learning. In the home, parents can supply children with proper diet and sufficient sleep. They can also provide learning activities, such as storytelling, reading a variety of written text, museum trips, and community sports. While such activities are more common in middle-class homes, labeling students as culturally deficient when they're unfamiliar with these activities hinders students' learning.

Since there is no child-rearing formula that guarantees total continuity with school curriculum or that guarantees successful academic achievement, we cannot make assumptions about students' home life. The goal cannot be to make the home congruent with the classroom. Although parents are children's primary teachers, they cannot be expected to conduct their home life like a classroom. Learning in the natural setting takes many forms, invisible to teachers and educators. Academic success is interactive and depends on much more than the family's home life. The students' home life can inform their learning and build continuity—one that enables students to reach their full academic potential.

Parent involvement is an ongoing process. It's subject to amending and restructuring as needed to strengthen connections between parents and teachers. Regardless of the form of parent involvement, one thing is certain: teachers must have the continuous support of parents, especially in culturally diverse classrooms. Parents help teachers help students achieve academic goals because they offer a great deal of information about their children and they can also share in the teachers' expectation for success.

Teacher-Parent Communication

Both written and verbal communications are the most critical forms of contact between the home and school. For effective teacher-parent communication, parents require knowledge of the language of the school. Conversely, the school personnel also have to make an effort to learn the language of the home or have translators available. Access to each other is restricted without a common language in place.

Effective communication with each other depends on both being available to deal with matters at hand. Nothing is quite as powerful as face-to-face communication. Meetings between parents and teachers as well as parental classroom observations are common sources of shared information about student progress. Although personal contact is the most direct type of parent involvement; it creates many difficulties for both sides. Time constraints are frequently cited as a reason for not contacting each other. Justifiably, teachers feel overwhelmed with daily classroom routines to contact parents during recesses and after school. Parents also have time constraints, which make it difficult to leave work or to receive phone calls at specific times from teachers.

Establishing strong relationships between the home and the school requires clear communication in the language that parents best understand (Hernández, 1997). Schools are responsible for ensuring continuous written contact through newsletters, notes, and bulletins in a language that parents speak. If written correspondence is sent home only in English, it is likely to impede communication with between parents and teachers. More and more principals and teachers recognize the importance of translating their written materials into the language of the home.

Parent Volunteers

Classroom volunteers enhance children's self-esteem because children feel valued seeing their parents care about their schoolwork. Parent and community volunteers also enrich the classroom curriculum with community talents.

Fundraising

This form of parent involvement requires specific skills. Parents have to have or be taught organizational, planning, and the time management skills to fundraise. Parents from culturally diverse groups may require training to organize such activities.

Policy Decision Making in School Committees

To participate in this way requires more technical knowledge about the operations of schools than any other form of parental involvement. Through systematic training, parents can learn about budgets, standardized tests, and decision making. Only with training can parents make informed decisions when they serve on district-level committees. Only with proper training are they able to represent the community's perspective as expected on policy committees.

PARENT EDUCATION

Essentially, parent education delineates a plan of classes, workshops, and conferences on such topics as literacy, child development, math, and other identified priorities. Parent education efforts can be of long or short duration, depending on the objectives set forth by the individual school or school district. Schools can make the training sessions accessible to parents in a language they best understand. Strategies for teaching parents incorporate a broad variety of ways that make the subject real and applicable to their lives. And the length of the training needs to match up with the time needed for the parents to integrate the subject matter. Ms. Kent's example, which follows, illustrates how a new teacher in a small, suburban school implemented literacy education for a small group of parents in her classroom. In turn, those parents taught other parents of students in her class.

CASE EXAMPLE

About Educating Parents

Ms. Kent enlisted the support of the strong LPC for diversifying her classroom curriculum. Then she implemented her plan:

> **Notice . . .**
>
> *How does parent literacy assist children in the classroom?*

I wrote a grant to a local foundation to buy
children's books for the parents and their children, books which the
families could take home. That's how I paid the child care student a

few dollars. An older sibling of one of the students in my third grade came to help care for the young children. First, I began by holding meetings in the evening twice a month and offering child care so it was easier for them to attend.

The training sessions lasted about one hour to one-and-a-half hours. Interactive formats included small group discussions, role-plays, simulations, demonstrations, and cooperative learning groups. After each class, parents had homework, which meant they had to read to their children and their children had to read to them. Here are some excerpts from the second parent class in one literacy training series:

Ms. Kent: I know that many of you already read to your children. But this time, we're going to focus on talking with your children about the stories you read and encouraging them to ask questions.

Mrs. Sanchez: I don't know why you want us to teach our children to ask questions.

Mr. Rico: In Mexico, we don't teach our children to ask us questions like the way that teachers want us to do here.

Ms. Kent: I realize that may be the case, but the part I feel most passionate about is for children to actively participate in their learning by asking the appropriate questions.

Mrs. Rosas: What Ms. Kent is saying is that our children have a better chance at knowing what they want to learn if they know what they're reading and what it means.

Ms. Kent: That's exactly what I mean. Your questions to me were fine, but you could add others, like, "How did the girls feel, having to go live with their aunt?"

After her first couple of suggestions, Ms. Kent asked the parents to suggest other questions that reached the characters' feelings as well as the reader's. She also wanted them to think about what might happen in the girls' new home with their aunt or how the situation might have been different.

Ms. Kent: These are all excellent questions. Mrs. Mora, please come up and write them on the board, and the rest of you also write them on your papers.

Parents wrote their suggested questions and read them aloud when asked to. They caught on quickly, and Ms. Kent offered her support by adding some comments to the parents' questions.

Ms. Kent: OK, let's read another section of the story. You're doing very well in the questions you're asking.

Parents Teach Parents

Ms. Kent commented on the group's progress: "At the end of the sixth training session, I knew that this group of parents was ready to train another group of parents. I sat in on their first two classes to give them support and confidence."

Mr. Rodriguez, Latino Parent Trainer, began with this introduction and summary:

> As Ms. Kent taught us, we can support each other. First, conduct sessions in Spanish because that's the primary language of the parents. Second, use language that people understand best. That means not using technical words unless we explain them in common language. Third, talk from our own experience, because we're experts of our own experience. Fourth, allow other parents to share their experiences. Fifth, validate their experience and ask them to share what they believe is most interesting about their group work. Sixth, allow the participants to demonstrate how they would teach a concept to someone else—public presentation skills. And seventh, use written handouts for the participants to take home, which will reinforce what they learned.

Mr. Rodriguez and his partner then talked to the five new parents about their expectations for the training classes (the conversation is translated from Spanish):

Mr. Rodriguez: Mrs. Luna and myself were trained by Ms. Kent and Mr. Garcia, along with other parents, and now we're here to share with you what we learned.

Mrs. Luna: If our children can learn to think and talk about stories, then they have a better chance of reading more advanced books.

Mrs. Velasquez: Will our classes be only about reading? Because my son is also having problems with math.

Mr. Rodriguez: Most of the classes will be about literacy, to help our children to think and question what they read. But we can also make time to talk about ways to help our children at home with math problems.

Following the second training session held by the parent trainers, Ms. Kent commented:

> I'm impressed by seeing the students reflecting what their parents have been helping them do in reading more critically. Certainly, it's a lot of work to train parents, but teaching is also difficult. And teachers need every parent's help.

Sharing family stories and finding other ways that parents can share their culture in the classroom builds family-school literacy. More important, it enriches the classroom curriculum.

Observations: Learning how to ask questions is as crucial for students to learn as knowing how to answer. The teacher's role in training parents to work with their children is primary. Although it is a time-consuming endeavor, teaching parents how to ask their children questions helps build a critical skill for the students.

Comments

Unquestionably, parental involvement and home-school partnerships play a major role in students' academic life. Affluent communities tend to have stronger family involvement than schools in economically distressed areas. European Americans parents are more visible and knowledgeable about schools. They participate more than parents from nonmainstream groups because they're more familiar with the school system. Although parents from culturally diverse groups are less involved, they care very much about their children's schooling. Lack of parental participation is due largely to inconvenient work schedules and lack of familiarity with the school system. In spite of that, in the home, parents hold high expectations for their children's success and expect them to respect their teachers. In so doing, they do their best to meet the schools' demands by helping their children to do homework.

The way that family and school relationships are built correlates with the socioeconomic and ethnic composition of the student body. One of the most successful ways of bridging such gaps is for schools to reach out to underrepresented families. Interested persons can co-lead parent-teacher training workshops and classes with teachers and other school personnel.

APPLICATIONS

▌ Application 1

Write a letter to the school board outlining how conventional parent involvement efforts can be augmented or changed to be more culturally inclusive, such as sending out communication in the home language.

▌ Application 2

If your school doesn't already have parent training classes, marshal resources to offer them.

REFLECTIONS

Reflection 1

Given that parental involvement in children's learning is critical, what is the strongest role that you can have in making the home and school connection a continuous part of the curriculum?

_____

_____

_____

_____

_____

Reflection 2

How can you build equity in the home-school partnership process when some parents are more vocal than others, and the school listens to those who visibly advocate for their children?

_____

_____

_____

_____

_____

PART II

Content

Learning Subject Matter
Through Culture in the Classroom

CHAPTER NINE

Teaching Cultural Diversity

> **I recall . . .**
>
> Translating for my father at the laborer's union where he worked taught me a great deal about the world outside of school, where I thought I worked hard to learn English. Going into dad's world built bridges between my father and me. It was an opportunity for him to talk to me about what he felt was injustice. His bottom line was always that my sisters and I had to stand up for ourselves because people would try to take advantage of us if we didn't speak English well. By sharing his frustration and distrust of the system, in his own way, dad was also helping to build bridges between the world and me, a world that I would later get to know very well.

Culture is relational: it exists only in relation to others in a given group. In this complex society, culture is constantly changing. It is always being shaped and re-created as it expands and makes contact with other cultures. People make sense of their lives through a cultural system (Bennett, 1999; Clayton, 2001; Spindler & Spindler, 1991). Cultural groups are in constant contact. While aspects of the traditional culture are maintained, more often, cultures braid together. Cultural patterns, beliefs, and attitudes are integrated because culture is learned and shared.

In the classroom, which is a cultural context, students respond to the teacher's expectations. For example, they know to remain quiet when the teacher is giving instructions. They know to walk, not run, inside the classroom and to turn in their homework at the beginning of the day. And they know to use soft voices inside the classroom. How students act out these classroom cultural norms depends on their interpretation of the rules. They reconcile what is learned out of school and how it relates to the classroom.

Teachers and students bring to the classroom a multitude of ideas, beliefs, and knowledge based on their own experiences. Classrooms are forums where open inquiry and diverse points of views can be expressed. Consistent with democratic values, teachers provide contexts where students learn a variety of perspectives, opinions, and beliefs.

Classroom teachers can motivate students to understand human freedom, justice, and equality through diverse cultural values. Such ideals, which shape a democratic society, are very much a part of the instructional program when the teacher delivers social science knowledge characteristic of students from different cultural and socioeconomic backgrounds.

Both the school and the family culture needs to intersect where children's schooling is concerned (Clayton, 2003). However, as school personnel, we cannot expect working-class, culturally diverse families to reject their culture and fit into a mainstream culture. What is needed is for educators to negotiate a common culture with the families—one allowing everyone participating to express themselves in meaningful ways.

As we've discussed, part of teaching is clarifying one's own cultural heritage and experience and how one's own culture intersects with other cultural groups (Ladson-Billings, 1999; Nieto, 1999). This means adopting positive attitudes toward differences. Recognizing the complexity of people, their lives, and interests makes it possible to transcend one's limited notions about a given group. We cannot limit our teaching about culture to that of the groups represented in our classrooms. It is equally imperative to teach other cultures and to connect them through their similarities. The aim is to incorporate as many groups as possible into the curriculum. This provides the global reality of humanity, understanding people's commonalties and differences on a broad scale, which is a fundamental premise of a multicultural curriculum.

By recognizing that all cultures have historical, social, and economic bases, we demystify the notion that cultural differences connote inferiority. Teachers hold the power to open students' minds about differences by teaching the *real* basis of culture. Thus teachers make connection with their own cultures as well as that of the students. Building bridges between cultures through effective teaching expands students' worlds while making it a smaller one. Such is the case with Ms. Carey and her third-grade class in the illustration that follows.

CASE EXAMPLE

Ms. Carey, Teacher

Ms. Carey had traveled some in her youth and during her college years. After graduating, she taught three years before returning to the university to work on her master's degree in literature. When she returned to teaching, inspired by her university classes, Ms. Carey organized her classroom to reflect the diverse cultures represented there, through books, artifacts, and pictures. Literature became a central medium for instruction. Her classroom contained mostly African American students with a few Latinos and European Americans.

> **Notice . . .**
>
> *How does the question strategy lead students to think about other cultures?*

Ms. Carey explains her background:

> I admit being rather sheltered when I went to do my undergraduate work and then my teaching credential. Having grown up in a very European American, middle-class, suburb city, our schools were mostly European American. We all bought our similar clothes that matched, from the same shops in the same shopping center, and ate similar meals about the same time because our fathers worked in the same office buildings and got home about the same time. Of course, there were a few minorities, but we never got to know about their backgrounds. Our classes never mentioned anything about them. That's just the way it was.
>
> I had traveled to other countries with my family. It was all part of a tourist package; and now I see that I never really had the opportunity to know the people. As tourists, we just saw other tourists in the hotels where we stayed. It wasn't until I was in my junior year in college that I got the opportunity to study in Costa Rica. There, a whole new world opened for me.
>
> That year in Costa Rica, I learned how difficult it was to learn a new language, even though I had studied Spanish for years in high school and one year in college. I'll never forget how much some of the locals laughed at my pronunciation, especially with words using the "rr." But my year in Costa Rica taught me how different and alike we all are. Their rich cultural values, the love for family, respect for others, and their kindness were so reassuring. I finally understood the importance of us learning other cultures.

Central to this knowledge, Ms. Carey learned about the way people live and what makes them real—their emotions, their thoughts, their joys, all those things. She learned that societies are similar in that there are poor and rich people everywhere. She saw that in Costa Rica, those who lived in the outer part of the cities didn't have it so good. In this lovely, green country, it was very tough when people had to travel to town on public transportation.

When Ms. Carey returned to the university to work on her master's degree, she felt even more strongly the changes that began for her in Costa Rica. Studying literatures from different cultures—American, English, European, African American, Chicano, Native American, Asian American— gave her a broad view of the world that she could bring to her classroom. She explains:

> I see myself as a cultural mediator, knowing the European American culture and my students' cultures. I've learned how our country is really set up according to the mainstream culture, and many have been shut out, intentionally and unintentionally. So I'm determined to help others see how the system works so that they know how to become a part of it. I show them how to function and live in both by knowing and appreciating European American cultural ways of doing things and respecting their own at the same time. What I like about teaching is sharing about the wonderful peoples of the world with my class and having them see themselves in other people. They quickly see that although we're all so different, we are also so much alike. Our emotions are the same around the world, even though we may dress differently, speak different languages, and even eat different foods.

A Classroom Lesson

One winter, Ms. Carey taught the students to work in groups, teaching them how to question, how to discuss, and mostly how to write by assisting each other with editing. She assigned some form of writing every day.

After reading about western African economics, animals, geography, music, dress, and art, including quilting, the class read *The Patchwork Quilt* (Flournoy, 1985). The quilt theme became a way of connecting the African quilt tradition and African American quilt traditions. The room was decorated with letters that students had exchanged with pen pals in different countries in Africa. There were one-page reports on the products grown in Africa and photographs of African fabrics from West Africa. A cord connected pictures of quilts from the African countries and African American quilts.

First, Ms. Carey has the class discuss *The Patchwork Quilt* all together:

Ms. Carey: After reading *The Patchwork Quilt*, I'm sure you have many thoughts and feelings about the book, but before you go to your respective small groups, let's brainstorm together to see what questions might help us learn more about Molly and her story.

Sarah: I have a question: What makes a quilt special?

(Ms. Carey writes the question on the board.)

Ms. Carey: Excellent question.

Jeffrey: Can grandfathers make quilts, too?

Ms. Carey: Yes, that question would make for good discussion, especially because we mostly see women and girls working on them.

Sonia: Ms. Carey, what about the patches, what if someone wants to make a quilt and they don't have old patches. Can they use new patches?

Ms. Carey: Good.

(Mrs. Carey writes the question on the board.)

Taylor: Do only black people make quilts?

Olivia: No, not only black people make quilts, 'cause my mother makes quilts, and she's Mexican.

Ms. Carey: Your questions are great. You get how this quilt actually touches all of us in some way. It isn't something that only one group makes, nor is it something that old people make. Young people do, and maybe even boys learn to make them, too. You get to dig deep into everything you know, what you've seen in your home, what you've read in school, even what you've seen on good programs on TV.

Olivia: I have another question. How long do quilts last? 'Cause the grandma in the story had hers so long that it was really dirty.

(Ms. Carey writes the question.)

Ms. Carey: That's a wonderful question. OK. These are all very good questions, and they're enough to get our group discussions going. Remember that after about a half-hour of discussion, you will each write at least a one-page essay of your personal ideas about the story, *The Patchwork Quilt*.

The students went to their respective groups to review the story as well and to discuss their thoughts about it. The groups were heterogeneous in

culture and gender as well as in skills. Each group decided to respond to whatever questions they wanted. Ms. Carey moved among the groups listening to their discussion and taking notes for the wrap-up.
Group 1's comments:

> "I don't think boys make quilts because I've never seen any."

> "Yeah, boys don't sew."

> "Ms. Carey says that boys sometimes do things we don't know about. Maybe they can make quilts and we just don't see them do it in the stories."

The students in Group 1 continued discussing how it was possible that boys and girls could quilt just as well as having quilts made for them by grandmothers.
Group 2's comments:

> "I wonder who taught the grandma to make the quilt."

> "Did her grandma teach her?"

> "Maybe, because that's the way it happens."

> "How do you know it wasn't her mother?"

> "I don't know."

Group 2's discussion continued probing into how people learn to quilt and who teaches them. They talked about how quilts belong to everyone because the patches of material come from different places.

> "Oh yeah, 'cause they got patches that belonged to everyone."

> "Yeah, and at the end, they didn't have a patch for grandma."

> "But when she was in bed getting well, they went into her room and cut a piece of her old quilt."

Group 3's comments:

> "Can we talk about, did all quilts come from Africa?"

> "Okay."

> "Well, I think that they began in Africa, and they were taken to other countries. That's how other people learned to make them."

"That sounds right. The quilt made its way around the world."

"Around the world?"

"How do you know they have quilts in every other country?"

"Well, if Judy's mom is Mexican and she makes quilts, don't you think Mexicans in Mexico make quilts?"

"That makes sense. How about China and Japan and Brazil? Do they make quilts?"

Group 3 continued discussing where to find the answer to the question about which countries in the world make quilts. Students shared about how family activities made them feel special, like when they play board games or when a father teaches the child how to play chess.

End of Class. Ms. Carey asked the groups to wind up their discussions and begin writing. The students wrote drafts of their essays and turned them in for the teacher to read. Ms. Carey shared her observations with the class:

> Your group discussions were super. I heard some very good comments about the quilts, their origins, their very special features, who makes them, and how they're as valuable in our lives as art. You have talked about the quilts as covers and as a way to learn from each other by sewing small pieces of cloth together that remind us of the special moments as a family, of holidays, of our family members, and how we have fun together.

At the end of the lesson, Ms. Carey encouraged the students to do more research in the library about other cultures in the world that make quilts. She urged them to continue to ask very good questions that keep them wondering and learning. The following day, Ms. Carey returned the drafts of the essays and instructed the students to read their drafts to their groups. Students then assisted each other with editing them.

Observations: By having students ask each other questions in independent discussion groups, Ms. Carey broadened their thinking about the way knowledge is shared: in class with each other, in families, and through quilt making and other family recreation rituals.

Comments

Connecting students to the cultural life shown in children's literature brings their family life into the classroom. Through literature, students can share ideas, beliefs, knowledge, and interests that shape their own personal lives. Ms. Carey teaches us that expanding our cultural horizons and perspectives through traveling, reading, and exploring, we can enrich our students. And learning grows.

APPLICATIONS

▌ Application 1

Work along with your students on a lesson to get in touch with their perceptions of people from diverse cultural groups. They can keep a notebook about their feelings, notions, and thoughts and share them with the class during a social studies lesson.

▌ Application 2

Create a class book project where you and all of the students contribute a brief description of something you learned from an older member of your family. Make a drawing or submit a photo to include in the book.

REFLECTIONS

Reflection 1

Discuss the pros and cons of the following positions as they pertain to your classroom: (1) all world cultures have a place in every classroom, (2) only the cultures represented in the classroom deserve priority, (3) only the European American mainstream culture should be taught in classrooms.

_____

_____

_____

_____

_____

Reflection 2

How do you describe the cultural perspectives that you present in your classroom through curriculum?

_____

_____

_____

_____

_____

CHAPTER TEN

Becoming Proficient in English

> **I recall . . .**
>
> I loved learning English in school because I was able to understand the teacher in class. But the fun part of learning English happened with a buddy who took me under her wing after school. Doreen was a classmate who invited me to walk home with her. All the way to her house, she became my personal tutor. She was quite a chatterbox, and to my ears, she talked a mile a minute. She pointed out things like donuts in the bakery, and then she'd have me repeat what she said. I repeated the words, and then she'd correct my pronunciation. At her house, Doreen's mother gave us milk and cookies. Then we went outside and tumbled around on her nicely mowed lawn. I always felt safe speaking English around her; even when she corrected me, it was playful. Many years later when I learned about "learning a second language," I realized the importance of Doreen's role in my early days of learning a new language. She made it emotionally safe for me to make mistakes and didn't evaluate or judge me as I stumbled in my pronunciation. She just kept inviting me over for milk, cookies, and somersaults on the grass.

Beyond question, students who speak languages other than English must learn English well enough to succeed academically in classrooms where only English is spoken. Even the No Child Left Behind Act (2002) makes this point. The Act refers to children who speak a language other than English, as do LEP students. However, every child has a personal internal clock for the length of time that they need to take to learn

English. Many students who are English learners speak their native languages at home and in their community, meaning that the classroom is probably the only place where they receive formal English instruction. Yet the ways teachers instruct LEP students varies greatly. For this reason, schools must establish a well-defined English program. It is not possible for LEP students to enter an all-English-speaking classroom and be expected to participate and compete successfully. They need a formal English Language Development (ELD) program to fully comprehend subject matter instruction.

English language learners in our classrooms come from families who provide different levels of support for the students' experience of learning a new language. Recent immigrants usually place high priority on their children's learning English in school. And while parents may want and expect their children to learn English, some may not know how to speak English well enough to help them. Nevertheless, they can assist children by setting a consistent structure at home.

Moving students through levels of English proficiency in the classroom takes several stages of language development. Hernández (1997) and Kottler and Kottler (2002) suggest several phases of language development for LEP children.

In the beginning stage, students may be hesitant to speak. They typically use nonverbal communication by pointing to objects and nodding or shaking the head instead of verbalizing a response to a question. Students rely on contextual cues, such as the teacher's gestures and body language, to understand the new tongue.

In the early production stage, comprehension increases, and students begin to speak. Students' vocabulary, grammar, reading, and writing skills improve. They may understand the main point of a story but will not necessarily understand every word. During this stage, teachers can provide students with rich, stimulating language learning environments.

In the speech-emergent stage, LEP students begin using descriptive words, and they begin to imitate conversations. They can do some summarizing of stories and lessons in their textbooks. Visual aids are still necessary in encouraging students to visualize and verbalize with greater ease.

In the intermediate fluency stage, students are able to express their ideas, opinions, and feelings. Their level of fluency indicates that they are translating less before they speak. Negotiating with fluent English speakers demonstrates their critical thinking skills, their abilities to analyze and evaluate. To support students in this stage, teachers can provide opportunities for students to make presentations and speeches.

In the highest level of English language fluency, LEP students are able to complete research reports and articulate ideas of higher abstraction.

The ELD levels tell us that miscommunication issues are part of learning a new language and not a time for penalizing students. In the classroom, what teachers may perceive as inattention on the part of students may actually be an issue of communication. Some students have a tendency to look away from the teacher while being addressed. We may think it's disrespectful for students not to look the teacher in the eye, but some cultures believe that being respectful means lowering the gaze. Such nonverbal communication is part of the larger picture of language in the classroom. And teachers must provide maximum support to LEP students to encourage their continued motivation in learning the language. The quicker that students learn the English language, the easier it will be for them to perform well in their subjects. Until then, LEP learners compete with native-language-speaking students who much more easily comprehend the subject matter. LEP students, spend years learning English to an equal level.

In some cases, teachers may perceive that children who speak a language other than English are not making a strong effort to learn the language. This situation occurs when teachers feel a great deal of pressure to have children speaking English as quickly as possible. The following example shows how Ms. Rivers attempts to work with her LEP students, with Chua, a Hmong student, as a particular focus.

CASE EXAMPLE

Chua, a third-grade Hmong girl in a small town near a state university, is the main character in this story. Although other Hmong children attended the same school, Chua caught my attention because she was the topic of discussion in the teachers' lunchroom. When the narrative begins, she had attended school for several weeks, since the beginning of the school year.

> **Notice . . .**
>
> *How could Ms. Rivers teach English to children who learn at a slower place than other children?*

Chua's family was part of a large refugee community that moved into this coastal town. The Christian churches in the area had sponsored them. Most of the families had been relocated in the community. Their cultural adjustment in this urban setting became more complicated than anyone had imagined. It was so foreign to these Kammu peoples from the highlands of Laos.

When the Hmong families first arrived in the United States, they attended classes that instructed them on some parts of the American culture. They learned ways to use American foods and about buying and wearing Western clothes, and they began to learn English. They were also taught how to live in homes with indoor plumbing and electricity. Hmong families could look to the east and imagine the green mountains of their former homeland. Although the serene landscape was stunning to look at, it was deceiving, because the Hmong were far from the rural lifestyle that they had left.

Schools in the area have generally been very helpful to the Hmong, especially those teachers who have learned some of the language to assist them in their cultural adjustment. But without adequate preparation in teaching English language learners, teachers who find themselves in situations like that of Ms. Rivers face terrible frustration. This situation calls for effective, systematic education in ELD.

In the Classroom

Here is what I observed:

Following the first morning recess, Ms. Rivers, the school's ELD teacher, divided her class into three groups. She sent one group to work on their English workbooks with the teacher assistant. The second group was assigned a story to read at their respective seats, and she kept the third group at her table near the windows. Seven Hmong, Latino, and Laotian students who were the least proficient English learners comprised this group. Ms. Rivers held up paper and pencil and told them to bring theirs. During the week prior, they had been working on conjugating first, second, and third person in the context of classroom materials. Ms. Rivers asked her group to sit in front of her, and she began with a greeting:

Ms. Rivers: How are you?

Group: Fine.

Ms. Rivers: Repeat after me, "I have a pencil and paper."

Group: I have a pencil and paper.

Mrs. Rivers: "You have pencil and paper."

Group: You have pencil and paper.

Mrs. Rivers: "They have pencils and paper."

Group: They have pencils and paper.

Mrs. Rivers: All right now, we're going to ask questions. Turn and get a partner. People facing that wall ask questions first. "Do you have paper and pencil?"

Students: Do you have paper and pencil?

Ms. Rivers:	All right; the other students answer, "No, I don't have paper." Do that now.
Students:	No, I don't have paper.
Ms. Rivers:	Chua, you're just sitting there; ask the question to Veto.
Chua:	I write on the paper with my pencil.

Ms. Rivers asked the students to recite a drill, which they repeated after her. The students had done this for weeks, since the classes began in early September. However, they were still unable to reproduce the English dialogue by themselves. During this group's time together, some children were more audible than others. Lucy and Chua's voices were barely audible at times. They spoke almost at whisper levels, whether they were sitting in a lesson or in playing with friends. Ms. Rivers asked the girls to raise their voices periodically during the lesson. However, upon hearing the teacher's voice, Chua turned away even farther. This muted her voice even more and prompted the teacher to continually ask her to speak up.

Ms. Rivers's Perspective

In the lunchroom, Ms. Rivers shared her frustration with two other classroom teachers about the LEP children who would not repeat the grammar drills. Conversations like the following one were typical as teachers managed to eat quick sandwiches while printing out worksheets for their afternoon lessons.

Ms. Rivers:	I don't know what to do with some of the LEP students. One of them won't even repeat the drills I give them.
Ms. Green:	Well, it's reasonable to expect that some students will need more time before they feel confident in expressing themselves verbally.
Mrs. Jacks:	Have you tried getting other kids to help her by sitting her next to someone who speaks English so that they can get her to talk more?
Ms. Rivers:	Yeah, they're all seated by good English speakers.
Mrs. Green:	Well, I know from my experience of teaching English learners that some students sometimes need more time to get used to the idea of being in a new country and learning new rules.
Ms. Rivers:	I agree with you, but it's been weeks since school started. Other kids are speaking up more in class. Maybe she's playing games to get attention.

Mrs. Jacks: Are you working extra with her?

Ms. Rivers: I tutor her like I tutor other kids after school. Today it'll be just her so I can hear her speak up. How else will I know what she's learning? I know some people keep them in during recess, but I don't keep her in. I need a break too!

After Class

As class was dismissed, Ms. Rivers called to Chua while holding up her hand like a stop sign. "Wait, wait. Don't leave." Chua put her head down on her desk until all of the students left. The teacher walked up to her and motioned to Chua with her hand to join her at the table by her desk. The teacher had simulated fruits on the table.

Ms. Rivers: Sit down, Chua. Say, "I see two apples."

Chua: (Whispers) I see two apples.

Ms. Rivers: Louder, say it louder, I can't hear you.

              (Chua begins to pout as the tears slide down her cheeks.)

Ms. Rivers: (Touches Chua's hand) Now don't cry, dear. You can do this. Let's try again. "I see two apples."

Chua: I see two apples.

Ms. Rivers: See? You can do it. Now, "I see two apples and two oranges."

Chua: I see two apples and two oranges.

Ms. Rivers continued drilling Chua to respond by mimicking her statements. When the teacher finished the drill lesson with Chua fifteen minutes later, she waved good-bye to Chua and instructed her to say, "Good-bye." Chua turned toward the teacher and whispered, "Good-bye." Ms. Rivers walked her to the door where Chua's siblings waited. She told them to talk to Chua in English so she could practice more. Chua and her siblings walked and conversed in Hmong as they made their way home.

Ms. Rivers had not met personally with Chua's parents, but she did talk with the community liaison who spoke Hmong. She instructed the liaison on ways that parents could help their children at home. Ms. Rivers was well aware that the parents did not speak English, but she suggested ways that they could help the children learn English faster—for example, to have them read aloud to the parents even if the parents did not understand the language. She also suggested that the children could watch good programs on television and that they do their homework to practice English.

The community liaison sometimes made home visits on behalf of the teachers. However, on questions like English language development, parents were invited to come to the school where the liaison met with them to present the school's goals. The Hmong parents were willing to cooperate with the school on all matters, but to the liaison, they confided their distress. The cultural discontinuity between the Hmong ways and the school's expectations stressed the families greatly.

Parents' Perspective

The Hmong parents, like their children, felt the cultural pressure from the school to change their ways. Through the voice of a translator, Chua's mother spoke about her family's tribulations and the difficulty of learning English in their new country.

> Our children go to school and learn to speak English. Teachers don't think that they speak enough English, but they do learn it very quickly for us. Even though they are learning English, their teachers say that they don't understand their textbooks and how to do their homework. The teachers don't know how much trouble it is for us Kammu parents. We don't know about schools here, nor do we speak English. The parents don't know what it is that we are supposed to do. The teachers tell us that we are supposed to support our children. But to us, that means that we are to have a place for them to sleep and to clothe them and feed them when they are hungry. For many of us, we are learning how to use American food, because we cannot grow our own food here. Here is only an apartment that has no place to grow anything.

The Hmong parents spoke about the concept of support. They knew about the notion because teachers had talked about the idea of parents helping children in the home. Space at home for children to do their homework seemed out of the question, since two or more large families usually shared a two-bedroom apartment. The parents did not know how to buy books for their children, but they told the teachers that they were willing to learn how to do whatever their children needed.

Chua's mother continued:

> Our children want to be happy here. They want to have friends, but that means that they get many new ideas that are different than the ideas we want them to have about our culture. Here we are told that people have to be left alone—that they must work by themselves—and

that they have to be strong individuals. Our culture tells us that we are to help each other. And we also want to help the teachers if they help us and show us how to do it.

> **Observations:** In her own words, Chua's mother showed us her wisdom about teaching and learning. She was the real teacher in this case. She had a wealth of Hmong cultural information for how to transform the ELD program—by "helping each other." Chua's mother was a willing and untapped asset in bridging the cultures of home and school for Chua, who needed a great deal of emotional support in learning English.

Comments

The Hmong children, much like other immigrants, required an extended period of time, a well-designed ELD program and supportive classroom and home environments as they learned to communicate in a new language.

The Hmong, as happens with immigrants from lower socioeconomic backgrounds, faced economic as well as cultural adjustment difficulties. Adults came to the United States without formal education or work skills. This restricted their employment opportunities. If students, on the other hand, meet with success early enough, they are more likely to remain in school, making an ELD critical. If students have not succeeded in school, parents are more inclined to expect them to marry in their early adolescent years. School personnel feel powerless to advise students otherwise. Such discontinuities between family and school expectations have been the domain of community centers in highly impacted Hmong communities. Health and community workers worked closely with school personnel on behalf of the children and families.

One of the discontinuities between the Hmong children and the schools is that their parents cannot provide them with adequate English language support. However, that does not mean that teachers cannot be successful in teaching their Hmong and other language speakers. Hmong parents want their children to succeed in learning the language and culture in the United States because this is now their home. The Hmong cannot return to their native land, and their children are the link to their future in their new country. In fact, some have thrived enough academically to earn doctorate degrees and become administrators in schools.

An effective ELD classroom program and a professionally prepared teacher to deliver the instruction are essential for creating equity for

English language learners. Learning English involves the students' emotions as they attempt to fit in and connect with their peers and a teacher who speak a different language. LEP students who learn English easily and in a timely manner have supportive programs at school and strong parental assistance at home.

APPLICATIONS

▌Application 1

Use multimodal instruction for LEP students so that they can use language that is more expressive with their peers during lessons and in turn, receive more support.

▌Application 2

Making the curriculum culturally appropriate helps LEP students in learning English. When teaching, relate information to students' background and experience. For example, in teaching something like the seasons of the year, we think in terms of four seasons, winter, spring, summer, and fall. However, in many places in the world, children only know dry and wet seasons.

REFLECTIONS

Reflection 1

Imagine sitting in a classroom learning about literature in a language that you have only heard spoken for three months. How would you want the teacher to approach the lesson in terms of pace, information provided, and delivery?

_____

_____

_____

_____

_____

_____

Reflection 2

Given that students progress faster in a strong ELD program when it's taught on a daily basis, what is the best possible utilization of support staff and other teaching colleagues?

_____

_____

_____

_____

_____

CHAPTER ELEVEN

Building Literacy

> **I recall . . .**
>
> Reading in school always made me nervous because when I could not speak English very well, the teacher always kept me in during recess, for a good part of the school year, until she was satisfied with my reading. What she never knew was that I was an excellent reader in Spanish. And at home, I loved reading in English. I would prop myself up against a wall and read for hours from the Colliers Encyclopedia books that mom bought for the family. From A through Z, I read each book and then started again. Even more fun were my favorite book characters. There was Pippi Longstocking and other fictional characters that transported me to new lands outside our one-room house. There were no strangers in my life. Books kept me company on rainy days and provided an escape during noisy times around the house. Unquestionably, my early experience with books has had a strong presence in my various professional roles. And over the years, in my research, I challenge the simplistic, deficit theories that portray poor and minority families as disinterested in reading.

*L*iteracy: There are as many different definitions as there are people who use the term. For me, *literacy* is a social and cultural process using and acknowledging the cognitive skills that are necessary for a student to interpret text. Literacy organizes the larger cultural system in the classroom, the family, and the community. Literacy is the tool of consciousness. Our oral and written traditions, what we read, how we read, and how we use it to relate to others, make up the powerful process. We become aware about our community and ourselves through this vehicle called literacy. The value of listening, speaking, reading, and writing has more than a narrowly functional purpose. It is a crucial means to obtain power and control over our lives (Shor & Freire, 1987).

To put in perspective this larger concept of literacy, we might consider a contrasting notion—that of "basic skill." Literacy in a basic skills framework separates reading and writing from subject matter. From this perspective, literacy is organized to teach the mechanics of reading first. Only after students have mastered the mechanics are they able to move into learning content in subject matter.

From what I call a critical perspective, literacy, reading, and writing are processes engaging students in verbal and nonverbal activities in their schools, families, and community. They inform students' learning. In the classroom, students can build on their past experience and incorporate new information with what they know. Classroom activities can provide students texts to read, interpret, and to respond to through writing. When teachers expand the social setting to incorporate students' cultural understanding, more learning occurs. And in classrooms with students who speak a language other than English, the ideal way of teaching literacy is through the language that the students know best. This is central to their literacy development. However, when that is not feasible because there are no materials in the students' language or teachers do not speak it, then it calls for the teacher to find knowledgeable people who speak the students' language. These could be peers in the classroom, older students in the same school, or community volunteers (Moll, 1990; Trueba, 1999).

The general principles which undergird the cultural perspective of literacy suggest that it is a basic tool and vehicle, enabling people to participate in society and obtain voice to advocate for them. Through literacy, we gather information and discover available alternatives. Through literacy, people information to make conscious choices for ways to conduct their lives. Literacy is a process designed by our content and is therefore malleable, every shifting and never ending. Literacy extends beyond written text; it includes one's knowledge about how to completely utilize innate power in socially constructed contexts. A person's ability to participate actively in a social environment shapes one's cultural knowledge (Au, 1993; Delgado-Gaitan, 2001; Vásquez, 2002).

Expanding literacy events culturally increases learning. The ability of teachers to assess their own cultural knowledge as well as that of their students determines the effectiveness of student-teacher and student-peer interaction. The example that follows illustrates how literacy is relational.

The Teacher's Background

Mr. Sanchez, a second-grade teacher in a middle-sized rural school, teaches a mixed class of Latino and European American students. His classroom is one of twelve in the K–5 school, which is located near the downtown area. He had experienced a great deal of success in teaching students who had not attained high literacy levels in their early school years. Mr. Sanchez attributed some of the students' achievement to his own joy of reading and writing, which he transmitted to them. His life story plays a central role his teaching. He explains:

> When I was a little kid growing up in this area, we all worked very hard in the fields. My brothers and I only helped in the summer, so we can't complain as much as my parents. My freedom from the heat and grind during those periods was to bury myself in a book in the evening. We sure didn't hear a bedtime story. My parents went to bed at sunset because they had to get up at dawn, but I tried to stay awake longer and read whatever book the migrant library had for us to check out. I tell you, it was such a treat to read about kids who had other kinds of adventures that seem much more fun than what we did in the summer.

Mr. Sanchez attributes his love of reading and writing to the opportunity his teachers provided in school. His teachers recognized his willingness to work hard to overcome his limitations in language and subject matter. By so doing, he was spared the label of "low achiever."

> Once I took off, I really took off. It was about junior high when I got to take classes that taught more literature, and that was so great. I particularly liked American literature, but when Chicano studies developed in the colleges, I couldn't get enough of the new literature by Chicanos. It spoke to the heart of my experience. And when I got to be a teacher, it was the most natural thing in the world for me to teach as though kids love to read and write, especially if the subject involves their personal experience.

In his classroom, Mr. Sanchez begins teaching children where they are at any given time. From there, he shows them how to think about what they're reading and writing. He sets the rules from the first day of school as to what he expects from them. And one of the most essential things he teaches is to question what they read and to ask questions about what they read. They also have to talk and share with each other, not just with him. Students learn what is significant about their literacy when they have to relate it to something in their experience. Mr. Sanchez's belief and teaching of literacy shows that in cases when children cannot find something in their own experience to relate to, they must find someone for whom the story is directly meaningful.

Literacy at Home

Like many teachers, Mr. Sanchez believes that if parents read to their children at home, children would become better readers. In Mr. Sanchez's class, composed of European American and Latino students, parents differed in their interactions with their children in book literacy activities. For example, most of the European Americans parents, who had been educated in American schools, knew to read to their children at all ages. For the most part, they did. However, in many Latino students' homes, the parents spoke primarily Spanish and felt unsure of their literacy skills beyond the early primary grades. Some Latino parents who did not read to their children engaged their young children in oral stories.

In their homes and community, students participate in many literacy activities, which educators may discount if they define literacy as a skill related to reading a book. In fact, students interact verbally and nonverbally with their family members and friends in ways that reflect their cultural practices.

A family literacy project was organized by Mr. Sanchez's school district. The project became one of the best bridges between home and school. A specific feature of the project involved parents in the leadership and planning. Maria Rosario and Antonia Suarez were two of the parents who assisted with the planning of family literacy classes.

Three premises steered the project. These were discussed at parent meetings as we talked about the issue and planned the development of the project: (1) All literacy is based on specific social practices, and (2) children become empowered through interaction with parents (3) and by reading stories that engage their personal experience. The discussions took place in Spanish. Here they are translated into English.

Many of the parents had participated in preschool workshops when their children went through the school district's bilingual preschool. They believed that during the reading activity with children, they could teach cultural knowledge based on their own experience. "There's so much that I want my child to learn, and they don't sit still unless I have a book to read to them," said Mrs. Duran. Until parents discussed these issues in parent groups, they were unaware of the cultural knowledge they shared with their children through reading together. Parents convey values, a worldview about their position in society, and a confidence to their children that they are valued. For example, in their conversations, the parents discovered that they all strongly valued cultural roots, extended family, and caring for others. These were values they wanted their children to learn. "I like books that help me to teach my children good values about being kind to others," explained Mrs. Morales. In the course of the project, the Latino parents became convinced that the more they read with their children, the better readers the children became as the teachers taught them.

As part of the literacy project, parents and children shared a story before bedtime. At home, children and their parents spoke in Spanish, and here the conversations are translated to English. In seven-year-old Monica's household, her parents said that they read to their children when they were young, but that the reading mostly stopped after they turned eight years old because the parents felt intimidated by the books that their children brought home.

Monica tugged on her father's arm. "Papi, you said you would read me my favorite book tonight."

Standing in the living room, he smiled at her, "You got me. Where is this favorite book of yours?"

"Here, it's this one."

"Let's sit down on the couch so we're both comfortable."

Mom called to the two older boys who sat watching television. "Boys, turn off the TV and get ready for bed."

"Papi, don't forget to show me the pictures when you read the story."

"OK!" Holding the book, he began reading *The Pink Elephants* in Spanish. Monica's father read the story of the elephants that liberated themselves and showed her the illustrations, one page at a time.

Monica's older brothers read their own books in their rooms, like they did every night since storytelling had become a regular event. On occasional Sundays, the entire family got together to hear the parents tell stories about growing up in Mexico. The family was comfortable with their storytelling.

Storytelling at home is often thought to be one of the most edifying events involving children and parents. As mentioned earlier, the central people in children's lives are their parents and teachers. Although these authorities sometimes find themselves at odds about what's best for children, storytelling at home is one activity that both believe is crucial to the development of language and literacy in children.

CASE EXAMPLE

Classroom Literacy Activities

In Mr. Sanchez's class, LEP students were placed in classes with native English speakers. Classroom literacy lessons typically moved at a fast and lively pace. Mr. Sanchez had grouped the students into units according to skills they shared, not their levels of reading ability. He worked with the groups separately on daily lessons.

> **Notice . . .**
>
> *How does the teacher incorporate students' experiences outside of school in the classroom discussion?*

To introduce a new story to be read, Mr. Sanchez began with asking the students of one group about any previous knowledge they had about the subject. In most cases, they spoke eagerly about personal knowledge and experience. Mr. Sanchez assisted them in organizing the content of their own stories into a sequence they understood. The students then answered questions about their own stories pertaining to "characters," "sequence," and "predictions."

Following these questions, the students were asked to read the new, assigned story either in the textbook or library literature book; they were reminded that the story they would be reading was much like their own stories, which they had just recounted verbally. The students proceeded to read the story silently. Mr. Sanchez reminded them to request assistance from each other with unfamiliar words. Meanwhile, he went to work with another group. After reading the story, Mr. Sanchez returned to the first group, and they collectively retold the story in their own words. Most of the time, they were able to relate the story in proper order with the correct characters as they appeared in the book. Mr. Sanchez then asked questions pertaining to the characters and how they related to other characters. The students compared and contrasted the characters and freely expressed their opinions and beliefs about the story: the funniest part, the saddest part, or the most unexpected part. Mr. Sanchez guided the discussion, but the students offered their thoughts with minimal prompting from him. Mr. Sanchez's role in literacy lessons was to help the students talk and express their views and understandings. In order to ensure this, he restrained his own opinions and listened to the students.

Discussing the Story

Eight students, a mixed group of Latino and European American backgrounds, had listened to a story about circus performing animals and a young boy who found a talented ant in the midst of the wild animals. He trained the ant to dance. After the reading, Mr. Sanchez began the discussion:

Mr. Sanchez: What's a circus?

Blanca: Is it where one goes to see animals?

Mr. Sanchez: Yes, but there are other places where one goes to see animals. How does the circus differ?

Maria: It's different because the animals are in cages and are tamed so that they don't hurt people.

Emily: It sounds like some of you have been to the circus. How many of you have been to one?

Mat:	I've never been to one, but I've seen them on TV.
Mr. Sanchez:	Those of you who know what a circus is, what animals does one find in the circus? You don't have to just direct your answer to me. I'd like you to ask each other questions, too.
Ellie:	There are elephants and horses, lions and other animals.
Mr. Sanchez:	What do the rest of you think about the animals we find in a circus?
Evan:	They're big!
Anthony:	Real big!
Mr. Sanchez:	True. Which animals do we find there?
Maria, Ellie, and Mat:	I've seen dogs who dance like ballerinas.
Mr. Sanchez:	Yes, sometimes they dress the animals to perform.
Mat:	I've seen tigers and those short horses.
Blanca:	Shetland pony's. That's what they're called.
Emily:	They're shaggy and short, like our horses in Mexico.
Mat:	You're crazy; horses aren't shaggy and short in Mexico. They're tall and strong.
Mr. Sanchez:	Maybe you've both seen different horses in Mexico.
Ramon:	Yeah, like circus. They all bring different animals.
Mr. Sanchez:	All of the animals you've mentioned are circus animals, but what size was the main creature in our story?
Whole Group:	An ant!
Maria:	Well, it was small, but it was strong.
Mat:	Yeah, it was tough.
Ellie:	And the boy, Tom, taught it to be smart.
Emily:	No, he was just trying to protect it from the other giant animals. He didn't want to teach it how to dance.
Ramon:	It was kind of a fantasy because ants don't dance.
Anthony:	No, it's fiction, not fantasy.
Mr. Sanchez:	Why do you say that it's fiction and not fantasy?
Blanca:	Because it's not true, but I think it's possible, so it's not fantasy. I think fantasy is like horses flying, but I think an ant can learn to move like Tom taught this little thing.

Emily:	No, that's crazy. Ants can't dance. No way. This is all fantasy.
Maria:	Mr. Sanchez, what's the answer? Don't you think it's a fantasy because it's impossible for ants to dance?
Mr. Sanchez:	You're raising excellent questions about the difference between fact, fiction and fantasy. Ask yourselves—what makes something real?
Blanca:	I know. Real is when you can see it and touch it.
Mat:	Yea, but it's got to be something that's normal. And ants don't dance. That's nor normal.
Mr. Sanchez:	What do the rest of you think? Does fiction have to be something you can see and touch? Is fantasy something that's not normal?

Mr. Sanchez quickly moved the group beyond the isolated facts that oftentimes confine a classroom literacy event. He began asking them questions that stretched their imaginations to think about the characteristics of fantasy and fiction. Of importance in this lesson is that Mr. Sanchez knew how to challenge his students, the kind who are often relegated to low reading groups that immerse them in the facts of a story because teachers believe that they may not understand higher-level thinking. In this classroom, students are urged to read beyond the words in the book and to question what they read.

Following this discussion, the group turned to their journals to explore their ideas about fantasy and fiction by writing about them. Although some of the students were unable to write extensively, they were given the opportunity to do so. Mr. Sanchez also surrounded them with assistance by seating the students together to share their skills. They were encouraged to ask for assistance in spelling and writing. The students continued their assignment the following day if they were not able to complete their work during the allocated time.

Writing About the Story

The students used personal journals to write about the books they read, especially their feelings about the stories. When the group shared their writings, they had written about things in their lives which they believed to be real and fantasy. One boy, for example, wrote that in his family, talking to pets was normal but that his friends thought that was dumb and strange. So he thought maybe ants can dance. One of the girls wrote that most of what we see on television is a lie, but everyone thinks it's true just because we see it. If TV is a lie but we watch it and believe it, then why can't we believe that Tom can teach an ant to dance?

Another part of the journal writing involved writing personal stories which had been shared orally with the group. During this phase of the literacy lesson, students began to understand that their written stories resembled those in the textbooks. For example, one student's eyes lit up when he realized that the stories he had written in his journal had endings like the ones he read in his textbook. Before this, he did not understand that a story actually had an ending. He pointed to his journal and commented, "I know where the ending is in the story in the book, because in mine, I know where my story ends."

In their journals, students were expected to write complete sentences so that when they reread their own stories, they would read smoothly. The students used words from the textbook stories that they found difficult, even though these words were not listed as potential new words in the textbook. New difficult words are often not the same ones that the textbook writers list in the assigned story.

Observations: Mr. Sanchez challenged his students to wrestle with fiction and fantasy by tapping into their own worlds outside of school.

Comments

Overall, integrating listening, speaking, reading (silently and orally), and writing, this second-grade class of Latino and European American students worked together. They collaborated in interactive reading groups because the teacher had a clear vision of what constituted a challenging literacy lesson. He expected students to excel by thinking critically and reading beyond the words in the book—across to other worlds.

APPLICATIONS

▌Application 1

Invite students to think critically about the stories they read by building in a simple question at the end of the reading discussion: "How would you change the ending in this story?"

▌Application 2

Many students may not have access to books that build problem-solving skills and critical thinking and present positive role models from various cultures, genders, ages, and socioeconomic levels. Organize a collection of books for students to check out by engaging colleagues, parents, and community members to contribute to a lending library.

REFLECTIONS

Reflection 1

What is your personal background in learning literacy? What part of your own learning process most influences your teaching of literacy?

_____

_____

_____

_____

_____

Reflection 2

Literacy from the critical perspective calls for students to learn reading for the purpose of making meaning of their world. How do you bring their world into the classroom literacy process?

_____

_____

_____

_____

_____

CHAPTER TWELVE

Creating Equity in Math and Science

> **I recall . . .**
>
> One of the most fun experiences I had teaching math was with a second-grade class. I had many students who had difficulty with even the most basic math computations, like addition, subtraction, and multiplication. I tried what I thought was every new program. Then I met with a couple of parents about their children's math problems. They said that they helped their children with their homework and they couldn't understand why they children were having problems with math since they always sent their children to the store to buy groceries and they always knew how to make change and returned home with the right amount of money. This gave me an idea. I asked a couple of teacher assistants who lived in the community to pay attention to children in the store and tell me what skills they used that would transfer to their math in the classroom. It turned out that the children who ran grocery store errands for their parents were quite capable in math skills. In the classroom, I set up an activity center that simulated a store. Students brought clean food cans and boxes. I brought in play money, a cash box, and other paraphernalia to make it a fun learning setting. Then I set out worksheets with computations that the students had to follow as they played merchant and customer roles in the "store activity center." The center was a great success for this class. The students were able to transfer their real-life skills to a math activity in the classroom and succeed academically.

Have you wondered how curriculum for robotics has robots engaging in competitions, and that they're often monsters? Monsters tend to appeal to boys, as does the competition style that engages monsters in fights. So what would engage girls in robotics? What if robotics were animal characters in the performance arts? The issues are about equity, access, and inclusion of girls and culturally diverse groups that have been left in the margins of math and science education. The gender issue in math and science has plagued schools as much as has educating culturally diverse students in these subjects. In teaching, we aim to help students overcome the effects of societal bias and discrimination. This is crucial if we're to make it possible for them to compete in a highly technical society.

In their book, *Radical Equations*, Robert Moses and E. Cobb, Jr. (2001) note that nearly 60% of new jobs now requires skills that only 22% of the computer-literate population possesses. By 2010, all jobs are expected to require significant technical skills. But groups, who have been weeded out of advanced math classes, including African Americans, compose only 2.6% of the engineering, computer science, and mathematics fields (p. 11). And advanced math is required for admission to college. Currently, the weeding is generally done according to performance in algebra classes.

There are two ways to address inequitable access to math and science: through science programs earmarked to advance girls and culturally diverse students in the subject and by designing challenging curriculum initiatives in math and science.

School district initiatives for increasing culturally diverse student enrollment and achievement in higher math and science classes involve students in a variety of activities. Programs typically operate after school, weekends, and summer vacations. They raise students' self-esteem and encourage higher career aspirations in addition to raising math and science problem-solving and higher-order thinking skills. The examples that follow are only two of many such programs that have successfully involved students from culturally diverse groups to succeed in higher math and science classes.

The national Qualitative Understanding and Amplifying Student Achievement and Reasoning project is a regional effort to increase ethnic and gender diversity in high-status math and science courses. It focuses on middle school Latino and African American students. Another national effort in improving math achievement of ethnically diverse students is EQUITY 2000. The College Board sponsored the program and it began in 1990. By 1996, the project grew to include over 500,000 students in 700 schools in fourteen school districts across the country (Gay, 2000). Students from the ethnic groups involved (Latinos, Asian American, African Americans, European Americans) have benefited from the program. They have passed high school algebra and geometry and improved their opportunities for advanced-placement programs in high school. The IMPACT project assists girls and culturally different students in their math and science achievement. This national project improved the assessment and achievement of Vietnamese, Korean Americans, Middle Easterners, Latinos, African Americans, Asian Americans, Haitians, and European Americans. In Chicago, the math leadership program led to changes in identifying and activating resources (Gay, 2000; Spillane, Diamond, Walker, Halverson, & Jita, 2001).

Culturally responsive math and science curriculum and pedagogy entails higher-order thinking skills and high achievement expectations for students. These goals are realized when the curriculum is delivered in a setting that enhances multiple learning skills. A learning environment that supports the equalizing of students' roles and abilities offers group work, fosters open-endedness and multiple intellectual abilities, enables common group products, and promotes individual accountability and academic activities that integrate subject matter.

TEACHING MATH

Culturally responsive pedagogy that enhances math learning for girls incorporates rigorous use of resources: materials, teacher-student interaction, and peer interaction. One program worthy of mention is referred to in Mr. Beck's example. He discusses adapting the complex instruction (CI) model of instruction to accommodate the multiple learning abilities in his classroom. Designed by the late professor of sociology of education at Stanford, Elizabeth Cohen (Cohen, 1994; Cohen, Lotan, Scarloss, & Arellano, 1999; Cohen et al., 1994), the CI model breaks classroom cultural patterns that have caused inequity in learning. With pedagogical models like CI, teachers are less inclined to show preferential treatment to students from a given culture (Clayton, 2003). A salient CI principle is that the more students participate in their learning, the more they learn (Cohen, 1994; Cohen & Lotan, 1995). The CI approach advocates that each small group of students work on a different task, using different resource and materials.

As recommended in CI, participatory instruction in heterogeneous groups develops conceptual learning abilities. Students learn to become active participants in their learning through increased peer interaction and varied roles assumed in their small groups. This is of particular significance for new students or students from any culture who learn best under guidance (Clayton, 2003). Participatory instruction is accomplished in small groups, and the teacher's role is transformed from authoritarian lecturer to knowledgeable facilitator. Research shows positive correlations have been achieved through highly positive peer interaction, challenging small-group tasks, and less direct teacher supervision (Newman, Griffin, & Cole, 1989; Rogoff, 1990; Vygotsky, 1978).

Mr. Beck's Classroom

Mr. Beck is a fifth-grade teacher in a small urban school. For years, he and other teachers in the school had tried to find a way to keep from placing LEP students in lower academic tracks where they have been restricted from using all their skills. These students had been typically kept in academically homogeneous classes, which did not allow them to interact with advanced students from whom they could learn. The slow tracks provided very low-level curriculum that did not challenge the students to expand their intelligence. The school had been aware of the limitations of the low academic tracks. Teacher expectations have been higher for students in the advanced tracks, which has perpetuated the disparity in academic outcomes.

Mr. Beck became concerned about LEP students' math and science learning when he recognized that many students knew more math than the test scores revealed. Most of the school's attention was being directed at the student's language learning. He and other colleagues began changing their classroom setting even though the school continued to track LEP students. His classroom differed from the traditional classroom because he insisted that students work together as much as possible. Different from conventional seat work, where students read and answer the teacher's questions individually, participatory learning settings encourage students to make higher-level-thinking connections to the subject of math. To break the pattern of tracking LEP students in his class, Mr. Beck, drew on the heterogeneous group component of the CI model.

CASE EXAMPLE

A System for Teaching Math

Notice . . .

How do the four groups of students in Mr. Beck's classroom arrive at their different solutions? How are they culturally responsive?

Mr. Beck explains:

I taught math to students in the low tracks. As I thought about how to change the students' learning setting, I signed up for a summer course on Complex Instruction (CI) training at Stanford University. CI went beyond the areas that frustrated me about cooperative teaching. For example, the textbooks and traditional curriculum and materials are not designed for small group instruction. Rarely do math textbooks provide small-group activities. The emphasis is on basic skills.

Mr. Beck appreciated that CI provided students the opportunity to work with peers. Through various group tasks, they can have different ways of understanding the main concepts of the unit. Students have diverse academic abilities in reading, writing, and math. Their intelligence comprises visual and special acuity, artistic and musical expression, reasoning, and verbal abilities. In CI, tasks are structured to get students who underachieve in academic performance to contribute more to the group since the tasks require multiple abilities. He continues:

> I had to adapt the approach somewhat, because ideally you work on the lesson until completed. And we can't do that. In this school, the recess bell governs the school day. So we have to stop the lesson and return to it the following day. After recess, we have to move on to a different project. Nevertheless, I use the heterogeneous, interactive group system to teach math and other subjects as much as possible. For example, as the teacher, I have to delegate responsibility to the students as a group and as individuals. I have to encourage the students to talk to each other, to support and to inform each other by asking good questions of each other. I'm strict. Students are responsible for their own behavior. They work in teams, so they're also responsible for their team's behavior as a group. But they continue to impress me with the respect they show each other. I never saw that when they worked individually. The process has taught me a lot, too, about how much I assumed about the students before. An eye-opener for me has been that in a couple of cases, I thought that the students were "slow" or "unmotivated." But actually, they were really just bored. When they had the opportunity to talk and work with others, they showed their true leadership.

Mr. Beck's Classroom Setting

For a person entering Mr. Beck's fifth-grade math classroom, there is little question as to what is expected of all students. Large cardboard signs hang on bulletin boards detailing the interactive organizational structure. Group norms and student roles are specified alongside the Activity Flow Chart, which delineates the daily activity for each group. Every student's name appears next to a group number and under the designated role they are to assume that day.

Students consult the chart when they enter the room and sit down to listen to Mr. Beck introduce the tasks for each group. The workstations are set in tables arranged in a square so that students face each other. Mr. Beck calls the students' attention to the large letters on the Activity Chart which state, *"No one will have all of the abilities required for the task. Everyone will have some of the necessary abilities."*

Group Norms

1. You have the right to ask anyone in your group for help.

2. You have the duty to assist the people in your group.

3. Everyone contributes.

4. Everyone cleans up.

5. Help other group members without doing their work for them.

Student Roles

Facilitator

- Makes sure everyone understands the task
- Calls the teacher to the group when the group has a question or a problem that everyone has attempted to answer or address
- Keeps time

Reporter

- Reports to the class about the group's investigation
- Provides context to help others understand the group report

Recorder

- Takes notes of the group's discussion
- Summarizes the group's investigation
- Compiles everyone's contributions into the group's final written product

Materials Manager

- Secures all materials for the group's investigation
- Collects additional resource materials (e.g., textbooks, other resource books, dictionary, rulers, magazines)
- Monitors the organization of materials
- Involves all group members in setup and cleanup of materials

Facilitator

- Facilitates open group communication
- Helps resolve group conflict
- Encourages participation by all group members (e.g., asks task-related questions, requests clarification, solicits observation)

The Activity

Group Work Activity

Students must work together to solve a single task.

- Activity is organized around a central theme.
- Activity cards, placed by students in pockets on a chart as they engage in particular activities, show the flow of students and the particular groups that they're assigned to.

Introduction to the Task

Mr. Beck introduced the task by reminding them of the concepts of *area* and *perimeter*, with which they had been working. He posted this question to the groups: "Mrs. Brown was planning a large party for her grandfather's 100th birthday. She had only been able to get four large tables that had these dimensions: 80" L X 39" W X 39" H. How many people would Mrs. Brown be able to invite to the birthday party?" He reminded the students that each group would raise different questions and construct and organize their data differently. But the key thing was to justify the predictions given the dimensions of the tables they had to work with.

After five minutes of introducing the task, the groups went to their respective workplaces and spent about thirty-five minutes deliberating and writing their conclusions. Meanwhile, Mr. Beck walked around to check on each group, asking the students questions and answering theirs.

Group 1 discussed the length of the tables if they were arranged in a U shape. They decided that this way there would be more room for people to sit on both sides of the tables and people could see each other. But they had a problem trying to figure out how many people could fit. Some of the students thought that probably only older people would come and some of them would be in wheelchairs. Other students said that lots of the grandchildren would probably attend, and they would be small. Other students thought that people could sit at three tables and use one for food. They finally agreed that they would use all of the tables to seat the people. They created room for people of all ages. They allowed room for a few wheelchairs and a few children and the rest adults. Ultimately, they assigned every space certain inches based on their own seating arrangements in the classroom and how much space a chair took up.

Group 2 raised questions about how many chairs Mrs. Brown had, but then they remembered that it was the area and perimeters of the tables that they had to consider. Essentially, the students decided that one table would be for small people like children and the other three tables would be placed in a long row with people seated on both sides. They assumed that they were all adults. And if even if they were older children, they could sit down at the table, so everyone was allocated a space. They based this on the inches that their teacher's chair measured and thus calculated the number of possible guests that way.

Group 3 drew the tables in a number of positions and talked about the different ways that people could sit. For example, the tables could be placed in a T arrangement, and the guest of honor would be at the top of the T and the other guests would sit at the three tables that formed the vertical part of the T. The students pretty much agreed that they would accommodate everyone with the same amount of space. They allocated the same space per person, whether they were little or elderly or men or women. They used the adult-sized chair as their measure.

Group 4 argued quite a while about the kinds of people who would come, because if they were elderly, they would come with someone. That would mean that more people would have to be able to sit. Following all of their deliberations about the size of people who would sit at the tables, they agreed to make room for all adults. If there were any children, they would not be sitting with adults at the large tables since kids usually got a small card table in another room.

Class Wrap-Up

Mr. Beck walked around observing each group as they worked. At the end of the period, each group spent ten minutes delivering a report. Mr. Beck asked each group to state the preconditions which they considered before concluding the number of guests based on the area and perimeters. There was little time for students to ask questions of each other. Mr. Beck deferred the rest of the wrap-up activity to the next day because it was a critical feature of their activity. It encourages students to engage with each other; it furthers the use of multiple intellectual abilities.

Mr. Beck's Comments

Mr. Beck reports:

Without question, the work involved for me, as the teacher, is worth the results. I've seen it work with students who were sinking in all of their subjects for a long time. They didn't understand it no matter how long they worked at it. One of the drawbacks of the way this school is structured is that we're still tied to the fifty-minute period. We have to stop, and then the students move on to another class. Sometimes we have to continue the discussions on the following day. Unfortunately, that breaks the momentum of the argument and the flow of ideas. As artificial as it may be, I still prefer to do it this way than to return to the tracking prisons.

Mr. Beck felt that not only had the students' academic performance and self-esteem improved but he also had changed and grown in his understanding. When students are placed in a challenging and engaging learning setting, they become independent learners. Their abilities are recognized while they are learning new ones from interacting with their peers who have different abilities and skills. In effect, even the underachieving students have to use language and literacy to learn math. They feel that they belong and can participate successfully.

> **Observations:** Each group approached the math problem differently. Yet each group's logic led to an appropriate solution. The students experienced the interrelationships that exist among math, language, and culture. They learned the tools to discover explanations of their own. And they learned self-reliance through the critical inquiry method.

SCIENCE IN THE CLASSROOM

Science, as much as math, is a critical subject in culturally diverse classrooms; science carries more weight than any other subject. Students from culturally diverse backgrounds have generally been left out of advanced science classes and career preparation toward careers in science. They have been poorly taught and as a result are unprepared for placement in advanced science classes when they reach high school and thus also excluded from college preparatory classes. Many curriculum initiatives are in operation to improve the science achievement of culturally diverse students with academic needs. Alaska, for example, has devised a culturally responsive approach involving Native Alaskan communities to empower their students in using the knowledge about their communities to understand science. Their highly collaborative process, involving community elders to help develop science standards, has effectively integrated indigenous and Western knowledge (Stevens, 2000).

Science as a Content Area

Culturally responsive science instruction integrates the students' knowledge and cultural experience with science skills. It assumes that students come to school with a particular set of beliefs, skills, and understandings from their experience in the world. The school recognizes the students' native knowledge. Based on this premise, students use their cultural experience to explore the world around them through observation and analysis.

Ms. Williams teaches fourth grade in a semirural school district. She is a seasoned teacher with quite a few years of experience. The school has an enrollment of nearly 600 students, most of who come from culturally diverse backgrounds and are bused to her school from nearby communities. Ms. Williams's training prepared her to teach in culturally diverse communities. In addition, the school had been focused for the past couple of years on raising the academic performance of culturally diverse students in literacy, math, and science. Reflecting the school's goals, Ms. Williams worked diligently on enriching her classroom math and science classroom to make it interdisciplinary and culturally relevant.

CASE EXAMPLE

Ms. Williams's Science Lesson

> **Notice . . .**
>
> *What are the strengths of Ms. Williams's culturally responsive science lesson?*

Ms. Williams plans her lessons so that four teams rotate activities weekly, until a particular science unit is completed, over approximately one month. She gives the teams a list of skills that she expects them to learn, like reading a weather map and tracking air pollution distribution across the country as well as locally, vocabulary such as *pollutants* and *sulfur dioxide* and *ozone* and *global health hazards*. Her science lessons cultivate collaboration between students, so that they recognize each other's knowledge and skills. The heterogeneous groups are composed of different students for each science unit. Students rotate their roles in each team as the teams rotate weekly until they have all had a turn at each activity:

1. *Motivator*: Encourages discussion and questions

2. *Note Taker*: Takes notes on students' discussion

3. *Facilitator*: Keeps time and checks with teacher when there are questions

4. *Manager:* Collects all materials for the group

5. *Reporter:* Reports to the class about the group's investigation

6. *Assessor:* Evaluates how students have worked

At the time they were observed, the groups made one rotation. They had spent one week working on different issues related to air pollution. While they were engaged in their respective group activities, Ms. Williams walked around the room, checking to ensure that students focused on the group's work. When students asked her questions about their resources or subjects, she often responded with a question. Ms. Williams believed that she had to make the students think carefully about what they were doing, guiding them to become independent learners. Once convinced that the students had exhausted their own avenues of thought and investigation, she assisted by pointing them in the direction where they could find their answers. For example, one student asked her, "Ms. Williams, our group can't find how it is that air pollution is measured. Do you know?" Ms. Williams responded, "What have you read? Have you checked the library books you took out yesterday? What do they tell you about techniques that environmental scientists use for measuring air pollution?" The students smiled and said, "Well, we probably don't know where to look." "What's the part of the book that would lead you to that specific topic?" The student responded, "Do you mean the table of contents or index?" Ms. Williams nodded and then asked, "Have you sent a team member to the computer lab?" Ms. William got the students to check the indexes, looking under "measuring air pollution" or "measuring air quality," not by giving answers but by posing question to help them to be resourceful.

Science Activity Teams

Team 1 Topic: "Research air pollution—visible and invisible types."

This team searched books and computer Web sites to explore their question of what air pollution is and where it's found. Students searched areas in the United States and in other parts of the world where family members lived. They also looked at the question of why some parts of the world have more air pollution than others.

Team 2 Topic: "Research local community impact of air pollution to health."

This team used books and computers to explore their question. They also invited a nurse from the community to speak to the class about local health problems resulting from air pollution, including pesticides, smog, and acid rain.

Team 3 Topic: "Conduct plant experiment to observe pollution damage."

To observe how plants are affected by pollution, students planted three bean plants and added solutions from an experiment kit that affect the plants differently (water, vinegar, and water-diluted vinegar). They watered the plants daily and observed their development while reading about pollution damage to the environment. Familiar words like *ozone, nitrogen oxides, sulfur dioxide,* and *carbon monoxide* became like second nature to the students.

Team 4 Topic: "Create a class mural to describe the global acid rain cycle."

There was no shortage of artists in this classroom. Each team took turns adding to the mural map showing the global acid rain cycle. Students used the world atlas as well as other world maps they found on the computer to identify the parts of the world most affected by air pollution and its extension, acid rain.

Class Discussion: Given that the teams spent a week on each topic, Ms. Williams held class discussions so that the teams could report on their different topics. The discussion took place after a recess break. On this day, Ms. Williams focused the discussion on the team studying how air pollution affected people's health. Ms. Williams encouraged the rest of the students to ask questions of that group. Ms. Williams explains:

> I try to have all of the teams report on a different topic so that everyone has the opportunity to report, answer questions from peers, and also ask questions of the other teams. So it's more than just knowing science. I want them to learn how to communicate it and to ask questions about it. Since all of the students have to take a turn at all of the four topics, they compile a rich body of information by the end of the month on the subject. You would think that there'd be a lot of overlap. There's surprisingly little, but they find some common ground even though each group poses different questions and has a unique way of getting to the information. The process works well. The class discussions get richer as the unit progresses because all the students get a chance to study the subject from each angle.

Here is a sample of the discussion:

Ms. Williams:	Team 1 Reporter and other team members, please come up here to the front and bring charts or notes, whatever you plant to use to help lead this discussion. What has your team discovered in these past days about the way air pollution affects health?
Jessica (Reporter):	There's a lot of information about how air pollution affects people's health. We read some pamphlets that came from the community health clinic. And in our area here, we have a lot of air pollution because of the agriculture and the pesticides on the crops and the smog that settles here because we're in a valley.
Ben:	So what does the air pollution do to people's health?
Jessica:	Well, we learned that lots of people were getting asthma. In our group, Gina talked about her family all having asthma. She can tell you about that, too.
Ethan:	How do you know it's caused by air pollution?
Jacob:	Actually, the medical information from the clinic says that a lot of asthma isn't caused by poor air, but once people get asthma, it's made worse by air pollution.
Nicole:	That's true, but what doctors have told our family is that our family's direct contact with pesticides in the fields probably caused the asthma.
Ryan:	There's another way that air pollution causes breathing problems. If people work where there are many smokers, the workers inhale the smoke and get lung cancer.
Ms. Williams:	Good point. Air pollution that affects us isn't just out there in the open air; it could be in our work places as in the fields and where tobacco smoke is allowed.
Jacob:	I have an aunt who lives in Mexico City, and my mother says that she got lung cancer from the pollution from cars and buses that all stopped on the street next to her little stand where she sold newspapers and magazines.
Isaiah:	We read that in other countries, the laws are not as strict for car smog pollution, so people breathe lots more car smog than we do in the United States. And airplanes pollute a lot. And some people are forced to live near airports because housing is cheaper. So they breathe more fumes. As the nurse from the clinic told us, these people who have to live in cheaper housing

are poor. And poor people don't have insurance, so they might be sick and not be able to get medical attention. So they're sick longer and sometimes die.

Ms. Williams: Those are important relationships between available housing, air pollution where poor people live, and lack of medical care for those people who don't have insurance.

Nicole: It's true that the United States has better regulation for cars, but in bigger cities, there are more cars than in smaller towns, and that makes a difference. I bet more people have asthma or other problems where there are more cars.

Ms. Williams: Excellent point. We cannot always assume that by regulating the smog control for cars or outlawing smoking in public spaces that it will eliminate the health problems caused by air pollution. Team 1, please help us to understand what air pollution hazards are in our homes that contribute to health problems.

The class continued for an additional half-hour discussing the topic of air pollution and its impact on people's health. Ms. Williams asked questions to draw out information that other groups had compiled.

Observations: Ms. Williams's multidisciplinary approach to science made the subject real for students. In her multitask method, students shared both the textbook information and also their personal anecdotes that brought science home. Through experimenting, computer inquiry, reading, writing, discussing, and asking each other real questions, students fully explored the air pollution science unit to consider local, national, and international health issues through deeper cultural understanding of themselves and other parts of the world.

Comments

Strategies for incorporating cultural diversity in math and science instruction create spaces for students to express their academic skills successfully. In a culturally responsive format, students learn from interaction that supports multiple perspectives, recognizes differences, raises conflicting opinions, and encourages students to resolve complex problems. They are encouraged to support one another's thinking and ideas. The teacher gives the message that there is no one single solution for a problem. In crafting learning contexts that appreciate student's multiple learning abilities, teachers must require students to assume responsibility for their learning. An interactive and participatory instruction becomes equitable when we build on students' existing knowledge and skills while embracing differences in thinking and learning. When students contribute just as much as they learn, equity ensues.

APPLICATIONS

▌Application 1

Design a math and science unit involving multiple intelligence abilities as described in the CI lesson.

▌Application 2

How would you assign student roles and organize groups in order to distribute roles for students in a math and science lesson?

REFLECTIONS

Reflection 1

How can you guard against having low expectations for students in math and science?

_____

_____

_____

_____

_____

_____

Reflection 2

Review a math and science lesson and identify the concepts that apply to the students' real-life experience.

_____

_____

_____

_____

_____

_____

Chapter Thirteen

Fostering Gender Equity

I recall . . .

There was never a dull moment growing up in a household of five sisters and, of course, my mother and father. It was a traditional Mexican immigrant household. My mother's words ring clear to this day: "Getting married is a choice. Having children is a choice. Taking your husband's name is a choice. But you better have your own checkbook because education and financial independence is your ticket to freedom." Mexican women are typically believed to be passive, uneducated, and disinterested in their children's education. And although I did not know what it all meant at the time, I knew she meant her words to make an imprint on me. And she always told my sisters and me to pursue a career and travel to many places in the world before getting married. These were all very strong words from a woman whose life was described so differently in U.S. history and literature books. But they very much shaped her daughters' lives.

In addition to our physical attributes, our thoughts, feelings, behaviors, and opportunities identify us as being either male or female. Our institutional practices still treat men and women differently in areas of employment, public policy, and presence in literature and in textbooks. Sports in schools have witnessed many changes in recent decades. However, more changes are needed to equalize the playing field for girls in schools, universities, and the workplace, which students eventually occupy. Diversity exists within every culture and within that variety, people respond differently to the world. Some of the variety in the ways that people respond and participate in the world around them is due to gender differences.

Therefore, our interest in equity must consider the complexity of gender differences as well as the overlap between gender and cultural differences.

The fact that much of gender identity is learned makes it a prominent issue in classroom curriculum. Old books, which are sometimes still used in classrooms, depict girls and women in simplistic and stereotypical forms. In them, girls are presented as incapable of doing the things that boys can do, including sports. Women were moms and performed housework while waiting for their husbands to return from the office.

Both boys and girls need to learn about gender equity. Inequality affects boys as well as girls. When one gender is confined to prescribed roles, it means that the other is also kept from expanding and broadening its horizons. When girls are restricted from participating in certain areas, in effect, boys lose, too (Sadker, 1999). Boys are sometimes singled out for misbehaving, while teachers call on girls more frequently. Girls are thought to be better students. Lisa Delpit (1996) writes that African American girls often have an advantage in classrooms where teachers perceive them as better behaved than African American male students. When teachers perceive African American boys as troublemakers, they are treated accordingly. Where boys may be classified as discipline problems more often than girls, girls are less represented in the high achievement ranks in subjects like math and science. Inequity also plays out in the attention that teachers show boys over girls in math and when answering questions.

Changes in the educational setting have happened gradually. About the same time that some elementary schools were beginning to integrate boy's and girl's recess lines, universities were beginning to organize women's studies programs. The advent of Title IX opened the general consciousness of educators. Equal treatment in order to provide equal opportunity in the school became the goal. In the mid-1970s, such efforts began to influence educators in the development of classroom curriculum and textbooks. They reflected a multidimensional representation of gender equity.

Classroom teachers were better supplied with materials to teach new values to their students about the true potential of women and their place in their communities, in history, and in literature. This was the goal one teacher had in shaping her curriculum on the theme of professions for her students.

Mrs. Yeh taught sixth grade in a small, urban community. During one spring, she told her class a story of the history of teachers. She described their strife, the horrific conditions, and the beliefs about women in that period of history when teachers were assigned to country schools. She assigned her class to write a report about a woman in U.S. history or in the present. Students were to focus on women's occupations or professions.

CASE EXAMPLE

Mrs. Yeh's Gender Curriculum

Mrs. Yeh felt strongly about the importance of gender equity:

Throughout the school year, I've talked to my students about breaking the stereotypes about girls and women. It seems that no matter how far the legislation has come about liberating women in the workplace, students still come to school with some rather preconceived notions about women's work. I'm always surprised at the kinds of comments that students make when the class is reading a story about a woman doctor or astronaut. Typically, boys that make comments like, "I didn't know girls could be astronauts. Or "I've never seen a lady doctor. Girls are nurses." I find myself stopping the story to do some serious attitude work with them.

Many of us agree that students are more aware these days that women are equal to men and are capable of performing almost any job men can do. But it never fails that students will have questions about the women's place in society. The majority culture views prevail strongly, beginning with mainstream media and parents' attitudes, which children adopt.

Mrs. Yeh continues:

As children we watch our mothers do so many things, yet we end up believing that women's work is of much less value than that of men. Women manage households, raise children, occupy professional positions, and hold service and skilled jobs. In my own family, my mother was a teacher. Then I became a teacher. But my father's job as a businessman always seemed so much bigger because the hours were variable. He had late meetings and so the attention was always on dad. My mother's job never called for that kind of attention; Mom was just supposed to be there to fill the gaps when he wasn't. She never told us that women's work was hard or that they did valuable work as teachers and attorneys and physicians. She just did it. We took her for granted. Anyway, I try to be conscientious about the way that I deal with issues of gender in the classroom. I know that they need to hear new messages loud and clear. I realize that no matter how much we know scientifically about the equality of the sexes, the cultural beliefs are far stronger and force us teachers to work harder to change those beliefs for our younger generation.

During International Women's month, Mrs. Yeh's class studied history and literature pertaining to women's lives. Most notably, she made the students recognize their attitudes about women in their own lives, women in different careers, and about their own potential careers.

Mrs. Yeh assisted her students in gathering books, magazine articles, and even videos on women's lives. She told them to discuss with each other how women's roles have changed over the years. Students had to account for what it took to make the historical changes that have transformed women's lives and the changes that remain to be made. Students collaborated on writing reports about issues facing contemporary women in contrast to women's past lives.

Students' Reports

> **Notice . . .**
>
> *How do the lessons presented here contribute to the students learning how these perspectives contribute to their understanding?*

Mrs. Yeh divided the students into four groups in heterogeneous mixes of reading abilities, genders, and cultural backgrounds. The groups discussed possible specific topics and selected one to research and write about. One group chose women's jobs, a second group chose women's fashions, a third group focused on appliances and conveniences in the home, and the fourth group chose women's images in books.

To prepare for their assignment, the class conducted long discussions after reading a book that told a story of three African American sisters and their European Americans friend who integrated a baseball league. The sisters' grandmother, who herself was involved with the segregated Negro leagues, added a great deal to the story. The students learned about the historical perspective of racial and gender segregation in this country. This set the stage for the class to discuss careers and job options for women.

Group 1 Topic: Women's Jobs

The students paired up to work on specific sections. They divided their writing and research tasks, often going to each other's homes to work on the project after school. Their research took them to libraries, the Internet, and personal interviews. The students divided the sections for writing their report. They talked about their writing process:

Jessica: We decided to write about women's jobs because we talked about it and we realized that all of our mothers had a job.

Ben: Our group divided the report into different sections; the first one about the jobs which women had earlier in this century, a second section about the women's movement, and the third section was about the jobs.

Ethan: I wanted to read about the kinds of jobs which women had a long time ago. So I went to the library and the librarian helped me to look up books that talked about the kinds of clothes which women wore and how many women made their own clothes. We could get to learn about the kinds of jobs which women did.

Nicole: We had to do research about the different jobs which women have, so I went to interview some of my parents' friends. That was fun. They told me lots of stuff about women's jobs and how they had lots of problems because in their work, there were mostly men.

Ryan: It was interesting for me to read about how women were fired from certain jobs after WWII when the men returned from the war.

Ethan: I still don't understand why the men got more jobs than women, but I know that's why we have to keep reading about this.

Group 2 Topic: Women's Fashions

This group discussed the issues involved in how women dressed in the past and how they dress now. Their research was conducted on the Internet and in current magazines, and some students interviewed store buyers of women's fashions.

Megan: Each one of us took a section that we wanted to study. Mrs. Yeh helped us with the research questions that we could investigate.

Kyle: It was kind of fun taking to women in the department stores who went to New York to buy dresses for women's departments. They have many decisions to make.

Syd: I feel bad that many women don't have money to buy the new clothes that are sold in department stores.

Sam: One article I read said that most of the fashions that women wear are designed by men. That didn't make me feel good.

Brandon: What some women told me was that it was much easier for women now than in the past when they had to dress only in dresses. Now women and girls can wear almost anything they want.

Maggie: One of the questions that our group had to discuss is the way that lots of women's clothes are advertised by skinny young girls in such a flashy way.

Syd: I think we learned that some of that is because they want women to look like the skinny models so that they'll buy the clothes.

Brandon: It still has to do with other people trying to tell women what to wear and how to wear it. It's not like the past, where women couldn't even wear pants, but now someone is still trying to tell women how they should look. My mother always says that this makes you wonder whether it is really freedom.

Group 3 Topic: Women Leaders in the Twentieth Century

This group read about the historical presence of women in the twentieth century. Each person in the group had to decide on a particular woman to write about. Most of the women they chose to report on were women whose names were unfamiliar to them.

Andrea: There have been so many women leaders in our history, but when we started working on this report, we could hardly find them in our textbooks. Mrs. Yeh helped us to see that we had to try to report about women from different cultural groups.

Paige: So we had to look in the library and the Internet, and we had to talk to community leaders. But we found quite a few. I wrote about a woman named Smella Lewis. She's an African American woman who was born in 1924 and fought racism and segregation and became an artist, and her work is shown in many places.

Mattie: I wrote about a woman named Madame Curie. I like science and medicine, and her life was really interesting. My father took me to the library and helped me find books about her life because we don't have a computer at home.

Ashley: My heroine was Harriet Tubman because of the way she helped so many slaves to freedom. Actually, there were quite few books on her and some textbooks had a little bit about her life.

Ray: I wrote my section on Dolores Huerta, who helped lead the United Farm Workers. She's been a real role model to many women to work hard and help people get their rights. There were some books that had some parts about her, but my sister took me to the UFW union office where I interviewed some of the people who work closely with her. That part was very interesting to me.

Jessie: My part of the report was about the many women who worked in the labor movement to make unions happen in different workplaces. One of my great-aunts worked in the garment industry, and she told me about some of these women's movements. It was all new to me to learn how so many women who made our clothes in the sweatshops had to fight to unionize. Before that, they would get hurt but no one cared because they didn't have insurance and couldn't get help. If they complained, they were fired.

Group 4 Topic: Women's Images in Books

The teacher assigned the students to make a giant, bulletin-board-sized collage with cut outs of women as they appeared in magazines. The students organized the magazines by types (e.g., glamour and fashion, science and news). Because they could not cut up books, they made copies of some pictures from their books and put them in the display. Students in this group wrote individual reports about their impressions of the way women and girls are depicted in magazines.

Community Presentations

A major part of this interdisciplinary and thematic unit involved Mrs. Yeh inviting women parents and community members to talk to the class about their jobs and careers. The intent was for the class to see the diverse roles that women play in society. Below are excerpts from some of the salient messages two of the invited guests had for this sixth-grade class.

The first guest, Dr. Calvo, was a physician and the aunt of a student in the class. Her talk raised essential questions about women in the labor force and the difficulty of succeeding. She brought a large chart to show the skeleton and organs of the body. Here are her comments:

> When I was in sixth grade like you are right now, I wasn't a very good student. I studied, and my parents tried to help me as much as possible, but there were ten children in our family, and we always had problems with money and illness with my father and although I tried my best, there were always many distractions. But when I went to high school, we were bused to a very good school where they had wonderful science labs and an excellent biology teacher. She was a terrific teacher and supported everyone in a wonderful way. I was hooked!
>
> One day she pulled me aside and asked me what I wanted to study in college. I told her that my parents couldn't afford paying for my college. She said that I was a good student in biology and that she would help me find a college and maybe get a scholarship to continue studying. I told her that actually I just wanted to become a nurse. She said that was fine but that I had to keep an open mind when I got to college and maybe get interested in medicine.

Dr. Calvo graduated and applied to numerous medical schools. Many women with whom she worked didn't do well and had a very hard time, but she didn't put up with any nonsense about being less than anyone.

> Already knew that's what I wanted to do, but I didn't decided to specialize in pediatrics until I was accepted to Stanford. By then, I had

worked and saved a bit of money, but I still needed financial assistance, and that's what good grades got me.

She reminded the students that good grades are necessary to get you scholarships, even this early in your schooling. And right now is when you begin paying attention to your grades so that you'll be able to get into the university and the job you want.

Balancing a career and family continues to be a constant juggling act, according to Dr. Calvo. She spoke candidly to the students about the demands on women when they marry partners who also have careers. All of it required careful planning and negotiating with her husband in order to maintain a household and care for their child.

Mrs. Phan, the next guest, was the mother of a boy in the class. She brought samples of the software that her company makes. She also brought an organizational chart to show the class the employees in her company and the line of command. Here's what Mrs. Phan told the class:

Although I was born in Vietnam, my parents left when I was a tiny baby, so I don't remember very much. Growing up here in this country, my parents learned English and wanted me to speak as much English as possible. I know a little bit of Vietnamese because my parents spoke it to each other. But mostly, they wanted my older brother and me to speak English so we could succeed in school. Even when I was in elementary school, I was so nervous that I might not know everything the teacher wanted me to know that I would stay up late and read my dictionary. I figured that at least I would know some words and their meanings. I ended up getting pretty good grades; I guess it was all the hard work and memorizing that I did.

My father was a businessman before he came to the United States, and he supported me in my decision to get into the business school at UC Berkeley. But I wasn't prepared for the prejudice that the business community has against women. That was very hard for me in college, but I talked to my father, and he helped me to get past some of the fear. After graduating from college, I worked in a couple of different companies that sold software, and I got promoted very quickly. So by the time I arrived at the current company, I had held many different positions, and they prepared me to be appointed president of this middle-sized company.

As president of the company, Mrs. Phan trains people in computers. She believes that women deserve to have a supportive place in which to work. She doesn't have many child care problems because her son Jeffrey is now old enough to get to his afterschool projects. But she still has to deal with all of the household business, and she likes having family dinners as often as possible. So she constantly juggles her work and family responsibilities. Although her work requires a great deal of time, her family life is her principal concern.

Mrs. Yeh's discussion about the guests' lessons started the students reflecting on the power, ability, and choices that young girls must exercise in their early school years and that their job is to focus on their studies and get good grades. The class responded enthusiastically to the guests as they talked about their lives in their work and their work in their lives. The questions that the students posed to the guests revealed their interest in the women's work. Both boys and girls raised questions about who took care of their children while they were at work. They also wanted to know how much money they made in their jobs.

> **Observations:** Mrs. Yeh's interdisciplinary curriculum exposed both boys and girls to a rich variety of women's cultural contributions to society and the day-to-day work involved for women to break out of conventional roles and move into professional arenas.

Comments

Learning about societal gender differences and the participation of women in different roles in society requires well-planned lessons to make students aware of women's multiple roles in this very complex culture. Another aspect of gender education calls attention to a fact that Mrs. Yeh wanted the students to understand—that in this society, women of different cultures have had different histories and different life opportunities than European American women. What makes lessons on gender roles like Mrs. Yeh's imperative is that most of the time, students live in a world that still undermines girls and women. Mrs. Yeh provides a rich opportunity for students to learn how gender roles are shaped in our everyday activities and how we can change the culture by how we interact with each other and the activities in which we engage.

APPLICATIONS

▌Application 1

Design a lesson where boys and girls discuss issues of debate for the class, such as girls participating in traditionally boys' sports. Have students write their perspectives.

▌ Application 2

The perceived notion that boys are free of the biases that girls experience is a disservice to both boys and girls. Have all of the students engage in a discussion, research project, and presentation about ways that gender bias affects boys and adult males. Have students examine stories, pictures, or games they play for biases.

REFLECTIONS

Reflection 1

How would you proceed to find out if there was discrimination against students in your classroom on the basis of gender, as opposed to race or cultural differences?

_____

_____

_____

_____

_____

Reflection 2

How do you know if you are achieving gender equity in your teaching?

_____

_____

_____

_____

_____

CHAPTER FOURTEEN

Crafting an Interdisciplinary Curriculum

I recall . . .

There was a time when team teaching and opening up the classrooms were the solutions of the day for the problem of underachievement, especially for linguistically and culturally diverse students. One of the best times I had as a teacher was in a third grade I taught in an urban city school; five other teachers joined me in what we called a "team-teaching pod." Each one of us was assigned a grade level, but we specialized in a particular subject, such as reading, writing, science, math, art, or social science for three different grades, first through third. I taught reading and was accountable for all of the first through third graders in that pod. All of the teachers planned together, and every unit we taught was coordinated because we used a thematic approach in all of our instruction.

The most challenging part of this endeavor was that as teachers we still had a lot of attachment to our "assigned students." When my colleagues and I met to plan our respective subjects, we often disagreed at first, so it took longer than if we only had had to plan for our own students. Stressful? Yes, indeed, but in the long run, students got to work to their potential in creative ways and advanced much faster than if we had to teach so many different ability levels by ourselves in single-teacher classrooms.

I n the past generation, we have seen serious efforts in the classroom to transcend the compartmentalization of subjects. A number of endeavors have encouraged integrating several subjects in the classroom. Integrating subject matter has been referred to as *thematic instruction, integrated curriculum, whole-language*, and *multicultural education*. Teachers often find it difficult to integrate subjects unless the school's philosophy supports it or encourages them to collaborate with colleagues.

Reading diverse cultural topics successfully makes connections possible between subjects such as writing, science, math, art, music, and social studies As part of the unique and shared history in the United States, the history, literature, contributions of diverse groups belongs in the curriculum throughout the year, not only on national holidays. The purpose for including diverse cultures in the mainstream curriculum is to depict the complexity of people's lives and the society. Portrayal of culture is fundamental. As I said in the beginning of the book, too often we rely on traditional, visible aspects of culture that create stereotypes about the people. Emphasizing only foods, clothing, dances, and crafts is a disservice to a cultural group, just as much as describing them through stereotypic customs. For example, typecasting an entire group in simplistic ways, such as "a particular group is cooperative" obscures that group's dignity and presents a falsehood (Huck & Kiefer, 2003). Cultural groups in the United States as well as in other parts of the world are influenced by their history, economics, language, and geography. Thus, the way any cultural group is depicted must take into account the complexities and identity of the people who belong to it.

There are numerous effective, multicultural approaches to teaching about cultures with integrity. Three major ones are usually employed: combined disciplines, thematic, and issue related. Combining disciplines can offer content-rich, interactive, and experiential methods of teaching about nonmainstream cultures that can enhance students' knowledge and appreciation of all peoples (Correa, Reyes-Blanes, & Rappaport, 1995). For example, teachers can design a unit on Chinese Americans and use history, economics, geography, art, music, literature, and environmental studies to inform the topic. In a thematic approach, teachers select a theme of interest to their age group—for example, community or changing bodies in adolescence. Emphasizing these themes teachers can draw on numerous perspectives to inform it. A third approach involves issues, such as the environment, bilingualism, health, or literacy in working-class communities. Lessons are built around a given issue presenting multiple perspectives from diverse cultural groups.

Using contemporary children's literature books, successful lessons can unfold on a specific topic involving a particular cultural group (Huck & Kiefer, 2003). From there, the theme can be threaded through other subjects. Such was the approach utilized by two teachers in a small rural-suburban coastal town.

Teachers' Planning

Mrs. Katie Jason and Ms. Beth Guy team taught a mixed fourth-grade through sixth-grade classroom. They divided teaching according to disciplines: Mrs. Jason typically taught math and science while Ms. Guy taught language arts and social studies. But

> **Notice . . .**
>
> *How do these two teachers combine their respective talents to design a cohesive lesson?*

often, the lines of expertise blurred since the teachers focused on themes to connect the various disciplines.

Mrs. Jason shared,

> We've been working as a team for almost ten years, and I can't overemphasize the importance of time in which teachers establish an effective working relationship. Beth and I have grown together, to the point where we are now. When we first began, we were more rigid about the way we divided disciplinary tasks, to ensure that students received the required time of the lessons in math, science, language arts, and social studies. One thing for sure is that our planning time has been the sustaining force of our thematic approach. We plan on Thursday for the following week. But even before we meet, each of us has done our research about where each student stands academically in the respective disciplines we teach. We have also researched the topics and tasks we plan to teach for the following week. That doesn't guarantee that we'll totally accept each other's ideas, but it gives us a more informed position from which to negotiate.

Ms. Guy commented,

> Although Katie's expert areas are math and science, if the students are acting out a debate in my class, they may have to incorporate math and science facts. They would then take time during their class with Katie to develop their points in order to deliver them in the debate during my class. For example, one thematic unit we've been working with involves Native American Indians. This combines their history and geography, dealing with their land, natural resources, culture, life stories, and science, which intertwine with the energy crisis and math. It also incorporates the demographic statistics of the tribal populations as well as their level of education and their economic conditions.

The plan was to cover a full scope of the Cheyenne past and present in order to get a broader understanding of the book, *Morning Star*,

Black Sun: The Northern Cheyenne Indians and America's Energy Crisis (Ashabranner & Conklin, 1982), which they read. The book was pivotal in combining many themes. But beyond the book, Mrs. Jason and Ms. Guy required the class to read other materials. The students conducted research on their own, using library resources for their papers and for a readers' theater performance, which culminated the project.

Interdisciplinary Approach

The book, *Morning Star, Black Sun: The Northern Cheyenne Indians and America's Energy Crisis* (Ashabranner & Conklin, 1982), tells the story of the Cheyenne Indians whose history has been one of defending their land from gold miners, settlers, and army troops. The movement of European American settlers westward infringed on their homeland for over a century, and it eventually restricted them to a reservation. Another century later, the Cheyenne faced another threat to their land when coal was discovered on their reservation. Many energy companies attempted to take control of the Cheyenne land to mine the coal. The threat was not only to the people's sovereignty but also to the environment, which faces irreparable damage.

Mrs. Jason and Ms. Guy's Classes

In preparation for the readers' theater, Ms. Guy divided the classes into six large groups of about ten students in each. Each group decided on a theme, which they collectively researched, discussed, wrote, and rehearsed to present to the whole school at an assembly. By this time, the students were adept at delegating responsibilities to each other and agreeing to cooperate as much as possible until the task was completed. The groups selected from a variety of topics: (1) early life of the Cheyenne tribe; (2) the tribe's religion and ways of healing; (3) Cheyenne life in the reservation; (4) the land and environment; (5) schooling for children; and (6) our own environment.

The students' readers' theater scripts were written and read in the first person, as if the Cheyenne were telling their own story. Ms. Guy edited their reports and extracted and compiled the parts that became the readers' theater presentations. The stories represented the research and discussions the students conducted. Following are excerpts for each of the groups' poignant stories. These samples were recorded during a rehearsal for the assembly. All of the students in the respective groups got to read parts of their presentation. Coordinating the timing where one left off and the next began was quite a job for the groups.

Group 1 Presentation: Early Life of the Cheyenne Tribe

In the middle of the seventeenth century, our people lived near the Missouri River. My people were one with all of nature, with the mystical powers of the sun, moon, wind, rain, thunder, lightning, and other natural elements. We treated the buffalo with great reverence. The buffalo as well as other animals, like deer, elk, wolves, and coyotes, had magical powers, just like the eagle and the hawk.

On the Great Plains, we the Cheyenne killed buffalo for our needs. We learned to ride horses from other Indians, and the North and South Dakotas became our home. Our chiefs were wise and brave and were good warriors. They cared about our people, especially those who lost their loved ones, like children who were left without parents. Our chiefs also had to be ready to fight for the tribe if there was a threat from outsiders.

Group 2 Presentation: The Tribe's Religion and Ways of Healing

Our sacred beliefs hold our community together. We know the Maheo is our creator who made everything: the sun, moon, stars, and the wind. He created people and put us here on earth to live with animals, buffalo, birds, fish, and other creatures that must be respected and never killed needlessly. Maheo has four sacred spirits, the north, south, east, and west—these are the spirits we pray to when we have a personal or tribal need which requires their strength.

The group continued discussing the beloved legends involving a prophet named Sweet Medicine. The name "Sweet Medicine" does not mean the same thing as modern medicine does; instead, it means bravery, strength, and goodness. The Cheyenne believed that this prophet taught them to listen and to do what was right for the tribe. During times of disaster, the Cheyenne believed that Sweet Medicine saved their lives because the tribe still had other work to do. When the prophet returned, he saw that their conditions had changed: the food was plentiful and their fighting among themselves had stopped. The group continued their presentation:

If we respect our nature, good things will come to us. We know that when we don't respect our land and our animals, we face suffering. There have been many times when hunters who came from outside our tribe killed our animals. In times of trouble, we still try to look to Maheo and pray that we find the peace that will solve our problems.

Group 3 Presentation: Cheyenne on the Reservation

In this presentation, we learned about the Cheyenne's life and the conditions prior to, during, and then after their life on the reservation. Before 1884 when they were moved to the reservation, they had ranged over 350 million acres. In the reservation, they had only a little more than 300,000 acres. When the people lived in Minnesota, they were farmers, but on the reservation, there was little rain, making farming difficult. For a long time the Cheyenne had to live on wild berries and fruits and whatever wild game they could hunt. They had very little beef that the Indian Bureau gave them—a small ration twice a month. But the Cheyenne were strong. Little by little, they began to adapt and find other ways to make a living. The students continued their presentation:

> Raising and caring for horses meant a new life for we Cheyenne who moved to the reservation in Oklahoma. Until the 1920s, we were able to call these "the good years" because the cattle increased in numbers and we were able to sell them for good prices. Our Cheyenne women canned fruit and vegetables, and we had a good diet even in the winter. We were able to build solid log cabins throughout the reservation. Although our people were poor, we felt hopeful.
>
> But a devastating blow befell our people. The Bureau of Indian Affairs killed our horses in order to make more grass available for the tribal cattle. Many horses were shot in the reservation and others were sent to other parts of the country. We Cheyenne did not receive much money for our horses. After most of the horses were taken, the Bureau of Indian Affairs separated us from the herd of cattle with a high fence so that we could not feed them. All we could do was watch them die in the cruel winter months that followed.

Group 4 Presentation: The Land and the Environment

> Our reservation was small but our land was beautiful. We respected our land and wanted to keep it as free from ruin as possible. Then the energy crisis came, which brought high oil prices to companies who use high levels of energy. Our reservation was caught in the middle of a major battle when the coal on our reservation made our land suddenly very valuable to outsiders. Once more, companies wanted to control us by buying the rights to mine our coal at the expense of our beautiful land.
>
> The reservation had a "Class One, pure-air rating." But the air quality was going to be ruined if the power companies got the

government to lower the rating enabling them to mine the coal for cheap prices. Those energy companies were not concerned about our land, the air quality, or our people.

Our Cheyenne leaders knew that we had to unite and prevent the companies and the government from taking control of our lands and mining our coal. The only thing to do was to stand up to them. The Tribal Council and other Cheyenne leaders met with government officials and energy companies to argue for keeping total control of our land.

Our Cheyenne leaders were able to convince the senator and the companies that our tribe needed the exclusive right to hire the company we wanted and who would respect our "Class-One pure-air rating" so that we could preserve our land. The Environmental Protection Agency had conducted their own tests on the air quality in case the government was to lower the rating. They found that indeed our Cheyenne land and the people would suffer if the rating was reduced and the mining was conducted. Our leaders won the appeal to the government not to change the rating. They were able to interview their own company who would honor our tribal wishes and respect our environment.

Group 5 Presentation: Schooling for Children

Historically our Cheyenne people have not had books or a system of writing or formal schools. Our mothers and fathers and other relatives taught us as children. Nothing was more important than being brought up as good boys and girls. We always had plenty of time for play. Our games usually involved pretending to hunt buffalo, to make camp or to surprise the enemy. As boys and girls we were taught to be excellent riders and good swimmers. Boys learned to use the bow and arrow from an early age and joined real buffalo hunts by the time they were in their early teens. Elders taught young boys how to go on their first war party. But as girls we were taught by our mothers to dress hides; gather firewood; make clothes, baskets pots; and to learn to keep camp.

The Indian Bureau, however, did not teach children as the elders did. The children were taken from their families and taught by teachers who wanted to make them like European American people. It was months before they could visit their families. Teachers refused to let the children speak their language. They punished the children if they heard them talk about their home or families. The Cheyenne children were not allowed to wear their traditional cultural attire because it was considered "bad." The students continued their presentation:

> Speaking Cheyenne would get us slapped. This continued until we began to learn a few words in English. It was good that we learned English, for that we were grateful, but the humiliation was too painful to bear. With every word of English we learned, we forgot more and more how to speak Cheyenne.

Group 6 Presentation: Our Own Environment

This group researched and presented their report on the present-day life of the Cheyenne who remain concerned about their land and are working to do as much as possible to keep their environment safe and clean.

> Those of us who are not Cheyenne or who don't live in reservations might not have coal in our back yards, but we are not safe from environmental pollution dangers. Our generation of young people has to become more aware of ways to care for our environment. Like the Cheyenne Indians, we cannot allow the destruction of our air, land, and water. We must do everything possible to make sure that energy companies, our communities, our families, and us as young people protect our resources. In our communities, we have started recycling; our families are participating by recycling paper, cans, and bottles. And as citizens we must read the newspapers and stay informed to make sure that there are laws that help to clean our air, land, and water from pollution. It's the most valuable lesson that we can learn from the Cheyenne.

Observations: For this class, learning about the life of the Cheyenne meant researching U.S. history, schooling practices, historical treaties, and their values for the land. And in so doing, they found common ground in the way that we all have to care for the land. Ms. Guy and Mrs. Jason's multigrade class is a rich approach to culturally responsive teaching.

Comments

Approaches to teaching cultural content in the curriculum can take a multitude of forms. The teachers, Ms. Guy and Mrs. Jason, represent only one style of content teaching that integrates a variety of subject matter in a multigrade arrangement. The small size of their school facilitates the interdisciplinary teaching. Through rich, interesting, and academically challenging activities, they stretch their students' critical thinking.

This culturally responsive instruction balances respect for the culture being taught as it presents the multidimensional life of the Cheyenne people. It also motivates students to question their attitudes about lifestyles of people different than themselves. Notably, it demystifies the life of other groups so that they do not appear exotic. Students can feel a connection to the fullness of these people's lives because they can see the mutual relationship to the real world that we all share.

APPLICATIONS

▌Application 1

Design an instructional unit focused on the issue of water conservation, integrating it through subjects such as science, math, geography, social studies, and language arts.

▌Application 2

Select a current concern from the newspaper that students can analyze for issues like cultural discrimination, stereotyping, profiling, or any other form of injustice. Beyond reading the newspaper article, divide students into three to five groups where each group takes charge of exploring the issue from a historical perspective or its impact on communities from a science perspective. Using a debate format, students can question people's rights on the issue from different positions.

REFLECTIONS

Reflection 1

What are strengths and challenges of teaching through interdisciplinary or thematic approaches?

_____

_____

_____

_____

_____

Reflection 2

Consider the curricular and classroom modifications involved in organizing your instruction in a thematic format.

_____

_____

_____

_____

_____

CHAPTER FIFTEEN

Conclusion

Responding Culturally in Teaching

Whether we teach in urban, suburban, or rural communities, we share the challenge to create inclusive, culturally responsive learning settings in the classroom. The teachers whose experiences informed and inspired this book have shown us their strengths and their vulnerable sides as they wrestled with their challenging situations. Faced with the enormous responsibility to respect students' cultures as well as to encourage them to learn about and in a new culture, we're forced to reach beyond our traditional resources. The teachers we met here taught us how to cast the net out to colleagues, the students' families, and the community leaders surrounding their schools. All of these players matter in providing students an equitable opportunity to achieve their highest potential.

No yardstick can measure cultural uniqueness. We must continually remind ourselves that no one culture is higher or lower, richer or poorer, greater or lesser than any other. One cannot say, for example, that Puerto Ricans have a better or worse life than Navahos.

All human conduct is culturally mediated. Culture shapes the way that people eat their meals, engage in politics, and trade in the marketplace, whether it's local fish on the pier or stocks and bonds on Wall Street.

Culture also forms the modes of writing prose, poetry, singing, enacting dramas, and raising children.

In all societies, children are born into an established family system composed of social relations, including parents, siblings, grandparents, aunts, uncles, and cousins. Extended systems of friends and peers are added to the network as children develop. It is a relational arrangement. In addition to the parental and extended family and community, institutions such as schools and legal institutions influence the children's roles in their cultural groups. These institutions, along with the family system, are major agents of socialization in society.

All societies have institutionalized means of rearing their young, of teaching them not merely skills but also a pattern of socially approved behaviors that guarantee their acceptance in their cultural community.

Children may seem to be only the recipients of the culture around them, but in fact, they too are active agents in creating the culture. Such a premise casts culture in a dynamic light, constantly changing and being recreated. Since most cultures do not exist as closed societies, they are contexts in which culture is negotiated when the players introduce new knowledge. By so doing, they reconfigure possibilities for resolving learning situations. Given that culture is not static or rigid, school is one context where rules, beliefs, and values are negotiable. Cultural diversity in our schools is vast. And educating students from many different backgrounds requires that we create negotiable contexts. By so doing, students have the opportunity to learn in more equitable settings.

When all students can achieve to their potentials in culturally responsive settings, we call that *equity*. A point worthy of mention here is that sometimes, students from linguistic and culturally diverse settings do excel in spite of tremendous adversity and prejudice. However, while some students survive such adversity, most fail under such conditions. The goal is to orient the learning setting to equitably serve the students from nondominant cultures. Educators are a critical force in helping students overcome the effects of societal bias. However, unless we work consciously to change bias to equity, we perpetuate inequalities in learning for children from diverse communities.

Designing linguistically and culturally responsive contexts and content takes as many directions and detours as our classrooms and schools dictate. Context that organizes the classroom content around interdisciplinary or crosscurricular themes scaffolds students' learning. Such settings support student participation in completing tasks otherwise beyond their reach.

CREATING CULTURALLY RESPONSIVE CONTEXTS

- Children learn their home culture through family interaction and peer relationships in play. Their leadership, language, and social skills transfer to the classroom.

- What we call *discipline* is culturally learned behavior. What schools call *discipline policies* are often culturally biased in favor of students from the mainstream culture.

- Exceptional students from culturally and linguistically diverse backgrounds exhibit intelligence and talents that deserve teacher, parent, and portfolio assessment beyond test scores.

- Inclusion of students with special needs in regular classrooms breaks the disproportional representation of students from culturally and linguistically diverse backgrounds in special education. Inclusion calls for multiple ability groupings as well as individual settings that utilize time and management strategies for assisting students with disabilities.

- High expectations characterize this aspect of culture. Both continuity and discontinuity are necessary in creating effective learning settings. Essentially, teachers' critical analysis of the students' family and community life, the organization of the classroom, and the students' academic standing determine how the students' culture gets either incorporated or changed in the classroom.

- Students' cultural identity plays a significant role in learning in a new culture. To facilitate their adjustment, it is necessary to incorporate their home cultures and make their learning meaningful.

- Parent and teacher communication enhances students' learning. Parents can participate in their children's education on many levels. However, in order to assist their children with schoolwork at home, parent education from teachers and other school personnel may be required.

CREATING CULTURALLY RESPONSIVE CONTENT

- Through literature books, cultural differences are taught in the classroom and bridge the distance between students and the community in which they live.

- A strong English Language Development (ELD) program is vital in the linguistic and academic achievement of culturally diverse students.

- Literacy that builds on linguistically and culturally diverse students' existing knowledge draws on their families, communities, and the world around them to make sense of written text.

- When math and science are demysti ed, learners who have been traditionally marginalized are integrated. Using their multiple intelligences and abilities builds critical and equitable environments.

- Making issues of gender explicit in curriculum content raises boys' and girls' consciousness about girls' role in society while making them all aware of their intellectual potential.

- Interdisciplinary thematic projects integrate students' multiple intelligences as well as cultural and linguistic backgrounds.

If there is no exact yardstick to measure cultural uniqueness, how do we know that we have created cultural inclusiveness and effective learning contexts and content? In the absence of a fail-proof method to evaluate effective inclusion and culturally responsive teaching, the key practice is to learn as much as possible about the students. Questioning existing paradigms, curriculum, and instructional strategies keeps you open to rethinking your approaches. The ability and potential of linguistically and culturally diverse students is evident only if we adapt formal testing instruments to include more in-depth assessment tools. As we've seen, children bring to school a wealth of information about their cultures, their families, and their communities. Utilizing these resources helps students make necessary connections in their learning. Acknowledging their rich cultural resources opens the connections and communication to the students' family life. Reaching out to these available resources keeps teachers from feeling isolated in creating culturally responsive classrooms. When teachers create integrated learning settings, students' opportunities to learn expand. True, this is everything but easy to do. However, the teachers in this book have taught us that it is not only possible, it's necessary and also promising. Every teacher in this book has illustrated the possibility for us to navigate the complexities in our own classrooms. They have crafted culturally respectful, academically challenging, and equitable learning solutions.

Now it's your turn, and I wish you great success.

References

Apple, M. (1986). *Teachers and texts: A political economy of class and gender relations in education.* New York: Routledge & Kegan Paul.

Apple, M. (1993). *Official knowledge: Democratic education in a conservative age.* New York: Routledge.

Ashabranner, B., & Conklin, P. (1982). *Morning star, black sun: The northern Cheyenne Indians and America's energy crisis.* New York: Dodd Mead.

Au, K. (1993). *Literacy instruction in multicultural settings.* Fort Worth, TX: Harcourt Brace Jovanovich.

Baldwin, A. Y. (Ed.). (2004). *Culturally diverse and underserved populations of gifted students.* Thousand Oaks, CA: Corwin Press.

Beals, R. L., & Hoijer, H. (1965). *An introduction to anthropology* (3rd ed.). New York: Crowell-Collier & Macmillan.

Bennett, C. (1999). *Comprehensive multicultural education.* Boston: Allyn & Bacon.

Bernstein, B. (1986). On pedagogic discourse. In J. D. Richardson (Ed.), *Handbook of theory and research for the sociology of education* (pp. 205–240). New York: Greenwood.

Bourdieu, P. (1977). Cultural reproduction and social reproduction. In J. Karabel & A. H. Halsey (Eds.), *Power and ideology in education* (pp. 487–511). New York: Oxford University Press.

Bourdieu, P., & Passeron, J. (1977). *Reproduction in education, society and culture.* Beverly Hills, CA: Sage.

Bronfenbrenner, U. (1973). *Two worlds of childhood: U.S. and U.S.S.R.* New York: Simon & Schuster.

Burnette, J. (1998, March). *Reducing the disproportionate representation of minority students in special education.* (ERIC/OSEP Digest E566). Arlington, VA: Council for Exceptional Children. Retrieved November 29, 2005, from http://ericec.org

Carnoy, M., & Levin, H. M. (1985). *Schooling and work in the democratic state.* Stanford, CA: Stanford University Press.

Civil Rights Project, Harvard University. (2003, January 30). *Minority children with disabilities.* Cambridge, MA: Author. Retrieved November 29, 2005, from http://www.civilrightsproject.harvard.edu

Clayton, J. B. (2001). *If we are not different, we will cease to exist.* Unpublished doctoral dissertation, University of California, Santa Cruz.

Clayton, J. B. (2003). *One classroom, many worlds: Teaching & learning in the cross-cultural classroom.* Portsmouth, NH: Heinemann.

Cohen, E. G. (1994). *Designing groupwork: Strategies for the heterogeneous classroom* (2nd ed.). New York: Teachers College Press.

Cohen, E., & Lotan, R. (1995). Producing equal status interaction in the heterogeneous classroom. *American Educational Research Journal, 72*(4), 99–120.

Cohen, E., Lotan, R., Scarloss, B., & Arellano, A. (1999). Complex instruction: Equity in cooperative learning classrooms. *Theory into Practice, 38*(2), 80–86.

Cohen, E. G., Lotan, R. A., Whitcomb, J. A., Balderrama, M. V., Cossey, R., & Swanson, P. E. (1994). Complex instruction: Higher-order heterogeneous classrooms. In S. Sharan (Ed.), *Handbook of cooperative learning methods* (pp. 82–96). Westport, CT: Greenwood.

Correa, V. I., Reyes-Blanes, M. E., & Rappaport, M. J. (1995). Minority issues. In R. H. Turnbull & A. P. Turnbull (Eds.), *Summary and analysis of reports of special education teacher trainers on outcomes and effectiveness of special education* (Report on Individuals With Disabilities Act). Washington, DC: National Council on Disability.

Darling-Hammond, L., & Bransford, J. (2005). *Preparing teachers for a changing world: What teachers should learn and be able to do.* San Francisco: Jossey-Bass.

Delgado-Gaitan, C. (2001). *The power of community: Mobilizing for family and schooling.* Denver, CO: Rowman & Littlefield.

Delgado Gaitan, C. (2004). *Involving Latino families in the schools.* Thousand Oaks, CA: Corwin Press.

Delgado-Gaitan, C., & Trueba, H. (1991). *Crossing cultural borders: Education for immigrant families in America.* London: Falmer.

Delpit, L. (1996). *Other people's children: Cultural conflict in the classroom.* New York: New Press.

Diss, R. E., & Buckley, P. K. (2005). *Developing family and community involvement skills through case studies and field experience.* Upper Saddle River, NJ: Pearson/ Merrill/Prentice Hall.

Epstein, J. L., & Sanders, M. G. (2002). Family, school, and community partnerships. In M. Bornstein (Ed.), *Handbook of parenting* (2nd ed.). Mahwah, NJ: Lawrence Erlbaum.

Epstein, J. L., Sanders, M. G., Simon, B. S., Salinas, K. C., Jansorn, N. R., & VanVoorhis, F. L. (2002). *School, family, and community partnerships: Your handbook for action.* Thousand Oaks, CA: Corwin Press.

Flournoy, V. (1985). *The patchwork quilt.* New York: Dial.

Foley, D. E. (1990). *Learning capitalist culture: Deep in the heart of Tejas.* Philadelphia: University of Pennsylvania Press.

Ford, D., & Harris, J. J. (1999). *Multicultural gifted education.* New York: Teachers College Press.

Freire, P. (1970). *Pedagogy of the oppressed.* New York: Continuum.

Freire, P. (1973). *Education for critical consciousness.* New York: Continuum.

Freire, P. (1987). *Literacy, reading the word and the world.* South Hadley, MA: Bergin & Garey.

Gardner, H. (1999). *Intelligence reframed: Multiple intelligences for the 21st century.* New York: Basic Books.

Gay, G. (2000). *Culturally responsive teaching: Theory, research, & practice.* New York: Teachers College Press.

Giroux, H. (1992). *Resisting difference: Cultural studies and the discourse of critical pedagogy.* Philadelphia: Routledge.

Hall, S. (1990). Cultural identity and diaspora. In J. Rutherford (Ed.), *Identity: Community, culture and difference* (pp. 222–237). London: Lawrence & Wisehart.

Heath, S. (1982). Questioning at home and at school: A comparative study. In G. Spindler (Ed.), *Doing the ethnography of schooling: Educational anthropology in action*. New York: Holt, Rinehart & Winston.

Heath, S. B. (1983). *Way with words*. Cambridge, UK: Cambridge University Press.

Hernández, H. (1997). *Teaching in multilingual classrooms. A teacher's guide to context, process, and content*. Columbus, OH: Merrill.

Huck, C. S., & Kiefer, B. (Eds.). (2003). *Children's literature n the elementary school*. New York: McGraw-Hill.

Individuals With Disabilities Education Act. (1990). P.L. 101–476, 20 U.S. C. ss1400et seq.

Johnson, B. V. (1981). *Russian American social mobility: An analysis of the achievement syndrome*. Saratoga, CA: Century Twenty-One Publishing.

Karten, T. J. (2005). *Inclusion strategies that work: Research-based methods for the classroom*. Thousand Oaks, CA: Corwin Press.

Kottler, E., & Kottler, J. (2002). *Children with limited English: Teaching strategies for the regular classroom* (2nd ed.). Thousand Oaks, CA: Corwin Press.

Ladson-Billings, G. (1999). Preparing teachers for diverse populations: A critical race theory perspective. In A. Iran-Nejd & P. D. Pearson (Eds.), *Review of research in education, 24*. Washington, DC: American Educational Research Association.

Laosa, L. (1983). Parent education, cultural pluralism and public policy: The uncertain connection. In R. Haskin & D. Adams (Eds.), *Parent education and policy* (pp. 331–345). Norwood, NJ: Aldine.

Lareau, A., & Shumar, W. (1996). The problems of individualism in family-school policies. *Sociology of Education* (Extra issue), 24–39.

Lewis, J. L., & Watson-Gegeo, K. A. (2005). Fictions of childhood: Toward a socio-historical approach to human development. *Ethos, 32*(1), 3–33.

Mahiri, J. (2004). *What they don't learn in school: Literacy in the lives of urban youth*. New York: Peter Lang.

Mohatt, G., & Erickson, F. (1982). Cultural organization of participation structures in two classrooms of Indian students. In G. Spindler (Ed.), *Doing the ethnography of schooling: Educational anthropology in action* (pp. 132–175). New York: Holt Rinehart & Winston.

Moll, L. C. (1990). *Vygotsky and education: Instructional implications and applications of sociohistorical psychology*. Cambridge, MA: Harvard University Press.

Moll, L. C., & González, N. (1997). Teachers as social scientists: Learning about culture from household research. In P. M. Hall (Ed.), *Race, ethnicity and multiculturalism* (Vol. 1, pp. 89–114). New York: Garland.

Montgomery, W. (2001). Creating culturally responsive, inclusive classrooms. *Teaching Exception Children, 33*(4), 4–9.

Moses, R. P., & Cobb, C. E., Jr. (2001). *Radical equations. Civil rights from Mississippi to the algebra project*. Boston: Beacon.

Newman, D., Griffin, P., & Cole, M. (1989). *The construction zone: Working for cognitive change in school*. Cambridge, UK: Cambridge University Press.

Nieto, S. (1999). *The light in their eyes: Creating multicultural learning communities*. New York: Teachers College Press.

No Child Left Behind Act of 2002. (2002). Retrieved November 29, 2005, from http://www.ed.gov/nclb

Ogbu, J. (1982). Cultural discontinuities and schooling. *Anthropology and Education Quarterly, 13*(4), 290–307.

Robertson, P., & Kushner, M. (with Starks, J., & Drescher, C.). (1994). An update of participation of culturally and linguistically diverse students in special education: The need for a research and policy agenda. *Bilingual Special Education Perspective, 14*(1), 3–9.

Robins, K., Lindsey, R., Lindsey, D., & Terrell, R. (2002). *Culturally proficient instruction: A guide for people who teach.* Thousand Oaks, CA: Corwin Press.

Rogoff, B. (1990). *Apprenticeship in thinking.* New York: Oxford University Press.

Sadker, D. (1999). Gender equity: Still knocking at the classroom door. *Educational Leadership, 56*(7), 22–28.

Sadowski, M. (2003). *Adolescents at school: Perspectives on youth, identity, and education.* Cambridge, MA: Harvard Education Press.

Shor, I. (1992). *Empowering education: Critical teaching for social change.* Chicago: University of Chicago Press.

Shor, I., & Freire, P. (1987). *A pedagogy for liberation: Dialogues on transforming education.* South Hadley, MA: Bergin & Garvey.

Sidky, H. (2003). *Perspectives on culture: A critical introduction to theory in cultural anthropology.* Upper Saddle River, NJ: Prentice Hall.

Spillane, J. P., Diamond, J. B., Walker, I. J., Halverson, R., & Jita, L. (2001). Urban school leadership for elementary science instruction: Identifying and activating resources in an undervalued school subject. *Journal of Research in Science Teaching, 38*(8), 918–940.

Spindler, G. (1977). Change and continuity in American core cultural values: An anthropological perspective. In G. D. DeRenzo (Ed.), *We the people: American character and social change* (pp. 20–40). Westport, CT: Greenwood.

Spindler, G. (Ed.). (1982). *Doing the ethnography of schooling: Educational anthropology in action.* New York: Holt, Rinehart & Winston.

Spindler, G. (1987). *Education and cultural process.* Prospect Heights, IL: Waveland.

Spindler, G., & Spindler, L. (1991). *The American cultural dialogue and its transmission.* Bristol, PA: Falmer.

Stein, S. J. (2005). *The culture of education policy.* New York: Teachers College Press.

Stevens, S. (2000). *Culturally responsive science curriculum.* Fairbanks: Alaska Science Consortium and the Alaska Rural Systematic Initiative.

Trueba, H. T. (1989). *Raising silent voices: Educating the linguistic minorities for the 21st century.* New York: Harper & Row.

Trueba, H. T. (1999). *Latinos unidos: From cultural diversity to political solidarity.* Denver, CO: Rowman & Littlefield.

Vásquez, O. A. (2002). *La clase mágica: Imagining optimal possibilities in a bilingual community of learners.* Mahwah, NJ: Lawrence Erlbaum.

Vygotsky, L. (1978). *Mind in society: The development of higher psychological processes.* Cambridge, MA: Harvard University Press.

Wood, J. W. (1998). *Adapting instruction to accommodate students in inclusive settings* (3rd ed.). Upper Saddle River, NJ: Merrill/Prentice Hall.

Index

**CORWIN
PRESS**